Student Guide to

ENGLISH
COMPOSITION
1001

2012–2014

D1303579

EDITORS

Joyce Malek

Cynthia Ris

Catherine O'Shea

Christina LaVecchia

University of Cincinnati

McMicken College of Arts and Sciences

HAYDEN
HM
McNEIL

ENGLISH COMPOSITION

ENGLISH
COMPOSITION
1001

Table of Contents

ACKNOWLEDGEMENTS

McMicken Hall

The *Student Guide to English Composition 1001* is the main textbook for students taking first-year composition through the McMicken College of Arts and Sciences at UC. Work on this version of the *Guide* started over two years ago when members of the University Composition Committee and the Composition Advisory Committee began drafting curricular goals and outcomes for each course in the composition sequence.

Members of the Composition Advisory Committee drafted, reviewed, revised, and reviewed again the assignments, activities, and microthemes that comprise the English 1001 curriculum. Each discussion helped shape the course and its possibilities.

The editors wish to acknowledge and thank the faculty who served on the UCOMP and CAC committees:

UCOMP

Sharon Burns, Jo Ann Thompson (Clermont College)
Maria Damen, Tami Phenix, Brenda Refaei (UC Blue Ash)
Frank Davis, Joyce Malek, Laura Micciche (A&S)
Pamela Bach, Barbara Macke (University Libraries)

CAC

Molly Brayman, Rebecca Borah, Chris Campagna, Les Kay, Christina La Vecchia, Joyce Malek, Laura Micciche, Catherine O'Shea, Jim Ridolfo, Cynthia Ris, and Hannah Rule

Thank you to Jessica Vieson, Devore Nixon, and Geri Hinkle-Wesseling for the skilled, patient, and good-humored administrative support they provide to the Department of English and Comparative Literature and to the Composition Program. They make our work better everyday.

Serving as models for imitation and discussion, student essays continue to be an important part of the *Guide*. We wish to acknowledge and thank the following students whose work you'll find in the last section of the *Guide*: Sarah Abellanida, Julia Fallon, Alexandra Land, Laura Plikerd, and Taylor Smith.

Thank you to the faculty who encouraged their students to submit writing: Lisa Becklehimer, Abigail Fagan, Michele Griegel-McCord, Patty Houston, and Megan Martin.

To Katherine Zlabek, Composition Program Graduate Student Mentor, whose photos of students and faculty you'll find throughout the Guide—thank you!

Congratulations and thank you to Brandon Whiting for his winning cover design. Check out the monkey on the back cover!

Lin Fantino and her staff at Hayden-McNeil have published the Student Guide since 2007. We are grateful for their professionalism and enthusiasm for our project. Each year, Hayden-McNeil supports our cover design contest with a $500.00 award to the winning designer. This year, we want to especially thank them for making it possible to edit the *Guide* online.

Finally, we want to thank Laura Micciche, Composition Program Director. For the past four years, Laura has led the Composition Program with energy, integrity, and dedication. Her expertise in the field and her commitment to collaboration has inspired our teaching and professional growth. The *Guide*, in large part, results from Laura's leadership.

The Editors

Catherine O'Shea, Cynthia Ris,
Christina LaVecchia, and Joyce Malek, Editors

Welcome to the *Student Guide to English Composition 1001*

The edition of the *Student Guide* you are now reading is the result of hundreds of hours of discussion and contributions over the past several years from faculty who teach in the English Composition Program at the University of Cincinnati. The first *Student Guide to English Composition 101* was published in fall 1999 and was joined the following year by the *Student Guide to English Composition 102*. In 2007, the two *Guides* were combined, and in 2012, the *Guide* changed again as we moved to a new semester-long course, Composition 1001.

Each year the *Guide* undergoes rethinking, revising, and editing as we strive to define our goals and develop materials that represent the writing and thinking valued throughout the many colleges that make up the University. As we continue to refine our curriculum, we welcome your comments on the *Guide* and how it functions with your assigned readings to develop cohesive instruction in writing.

WHAT'S IN THE *GUIDE*

The *Guide* is divided into several sections. The first three provide information and material related to the composition program and to college-level writing. The Guidelines and Forms section contains information about how your papers will be assessed, plagiarism information, and evaluation forms for you to fill out at the end of each term. Since writing from students is a critical part of the *Guide*, we include a Publication Consent Form for you to fill out if you would like us to consider any of your papers for publication in the next edition of the *Guide*. The final section introduces you to the Writing Center, a valuable resource for all student writers.

The next section of the *Guide* presents the curriculum for Composition 1001, complete with course requirements, goals, policies, assignment descriptions, and, where available, student essay examples for each assignment.

Composition 1001 introduces you to the kinds of analytic skills college students are expected to demonstrate as they read and respond to analytical and argument-based written, spoken, and visual texts. By the end of Composition 1001, you should be able to analyze and synthesize ideas while remaining aware of rhetorical concepts like audience, purpose, situation, and voice. Over the course of the semester you will also work with diverse Research Steps designed to help you find a topic that engages you, focus your research process, articulate a thesis, and plan out your argument. The writing from your Research Steps will help you compose your Researched Argument essay. After completing your Researched Argument, you will recast your essay into a new form, with a more public audience in mind. Last, your instructor will ask that you reflect on what you have learned about writing and about yourself as a writer, and also to analyze the ways in which your writing has changed from the beginning of the semester.

Writing is hard work. As such, we have attempted to provide you with a valuable tool to complement your instructor's approach to writing. All of us welcome you to the University of Cincinnati's writing program and wish you success in your college career.

The Editors

Sequence and Goals of the English Composition Requirement

English Composition is a university-wide required General Education course, which is designed to help you develop knowledge and skills to achieve the four Baccalaureate Competencies. The Baccalaureate Competencies are the critical abilities shared by all educated persons, and they comprise a major component of the General Education Program. The four Baccalaureate Competencies include: Critical Thinking, Effective Communication, Knowledge Integration, and Social Responsibility. In particular, English Composition focuses on **Critical Thinking** and **Effective Communication**.

Critical Thinking is the ability to analyze, synthesize, and evaluate information and ideas from multiple perspectives. The educated individual thinks critically and analytically about subjects. Critical thinking includes the capability for analysis, problem solving, logical argument, the application of scholarly and scientific methods, the accurate use of terminology, and information literacy. The particular critical thinking skills vary from discipline to discipline. **Effective Communication** embraces aural, visual, and language arts, including the ability to read, write, speak, and listen; it is the effective use of various resources and technology for personal and professional communication. The educated individual must be able to understand and convey ideas in diverse contexts, using appropriate communication and information technology resources and skills. Among important language capabilities are proper usage, appropriate style, and the ability to formulate a coherent, well-supported argument using language appropriate to academic and public discourse.

The English Composition course in which you are enrolled is the first course in a two-part sequence that has been carefully designed to help you develop both critical thinking and effective communication. These competencies are developed and honed over time, which is why we have sequenced these courses in the following manner and why the courses must be taken in order:

Course	Description	Goals
English 1001	English Composition 1001 emphasizes critical thinking and persuasive writing skills. Students learn to read critically and analyze a text's content as well as its rhetorical strategies. In addition, students are immersed in research writing practices, learning, for instance, how to integrate source material into their papers, evaluate sources, and position their ideas in relation to published research. The course aims to develop confident writers who know how to pursue and develop a relevant, consequential line of inquiry.	After successful completion of English Composition 1001, students should be able to: • Understand the complexity of different kinds of arguments/issues; • Recognize that different writing situations call for different strategies; • Recognize that texts are in conversation with other texts; • Understand and demonstrate the ethical responsibility of the research writer to explore multiple perspectives on a topic; • Understand and demonstrate the ethical responsibility of the research writer to cite sources and report findings accurately.

English 2089 Intermediate Composition	This intermediate, General Education course reinforces what students learn in first-year Composition, introduces higher-level learning about writing and reading, and focuses students' attention on how meaning is made, understood, and communicated across and within discourse communities. The course emphasizes critical reading and writing, advanced research and argumentative skills, and rhetorical sensitivity to differences in academic, professional, and/or public writing.	Building on skills developed in English Composition 1001, students successfully completing English 2089 should be able to do the following: • Demonstrate refined rhetorical awareness, including the ability to analyze, compare, and evaluate how rhetorical strategies function within various discourse communities, and to work with a variety of genres to understand how meaning is made, communicated, and debated in various contexts; • Demonstrate critical reading, writing, and thinking skills, including the ability to identify and distinguish among kinds of evidence used in discourse communities, to locate, evaluate, and integrate sources appropriate to research inquiry, and to produce clear, organized texts appropriate to situation, purpose, and audience; • Engage thoughtfully in the writing process, including the ability to write and revise drafts and integrate feedback into their own writing, as well as critique others' texts, to use flexible strategies for generating, revising, editing, and proofreading, and to understand the collaborative and social dimensions of the writing process; • Demonstrate knowledge of conventions across varying contexts, including the ability to use conventions of format, organization, and language, to use appropriate documentation and citation guidelines and styles, and to demonstrate that different genres may require distinct forms of citation, formatting, and documentation.

The assignments you complete in the English Composition courses will help you develop transferable skills that will contribute to your development of the Baccalaureate Competencies of critical thinking and effective communication.

English Composition Guiding Principles

We learn to write by writing. Writing competency is cumulative: it takes practice and more practice. Daily writing activities, formal and informal, are crucial to becoming a more fluent, confident writer.

Writing is the content of composition classes. Our goal as teachers is to help you express, in writing, increasingly complex ideas. We value writing that is clear, well-organized, rhetorically aware, and critically engaged. These attributes are not specific to composition courses, but are aspects of writing valued across and beyond the academic disciplines.

Writing is a process. Writing courses provide you with opportunities for invention, drafting, editing, revising, and reflection because thoughtful writing requires time and feedback. We recognize, however, that there is no single process that fits every writer; our teachers are attentive to your different learning styles and allow for appropriate flexibility.

Writing and revision go hand-in-hand. You will have opportunities for revision in each composition course. Revising requires that writers return to a draft, rethinking and reshaping what it says. We like Joseph Harris's description of revision in his book *Rewriting*: "The aim of revising should not be simply to fix up or refine a text but to develop and extend what it has to say—to make your writing more precise, nuanced, inventive, and surprising" (116). Adding, cutting, moving, rethinking, and reorganizing text—these are important moves for meaningful revision. Editing, or correcting errors and improving sentences for clarity and readability, is an important part of the writing process as well, but if the "big picture" of an essay is not developed and refined, then the sentence-level changes will not make a significant difference to the essay's overall success.

Writing happens in a community. UC writing classes provide opportunities for you to share your writing and to read and respond to your classmates' writing. Writing courses are not lectures, but are discussion-based courses that require your involvement and participation. Much of the writing that you will do in this community will be addressed to the academic community, as represented by your teacher and class. Writing for an academic community involves using accepted conventions of formal writing, avoiding slang, supporting your claim, developing your ideas, and providing context for your audience.

Writing courses teach you how to write well with *and* without teachers. You'll learn how to become better readers of your own writing through teacher instruction and feedback. However, we believe that you are not served well by an approach that places all responsibility for learning on the teacher. Thus, we foster independence in student-writers through activities like peer review, reflection, group work, and the expectation of ongoing revision and research. Our goal is for you to leave our classrooms with a good sense of how to generate ideas for a paper, organize them in a convincing and logical way, integrate relevant research, craft an appropriate voice for an audience and purpose, and edit and revise, based on self-assessment and reader feedback.

Writing courses are not grammar courses. Our charge in English Composition is to teach you how to craft cohesive essays of increasing complexity. While grammar competency is an integral component of writing performance, writers do not learn how to write by learning grammar rules. They learn how to write by writing and re-reading and re-writing.

Writing is an adventure! We hope that you'll learn something about yourself through the process of reading, thinking, and writing in our composition courses here at UC. Writing means discovering. Through a variety of writing tasks and activities, you can explore not only the subject matter of your work, but also your own thinking.

A Note about Revision

WHAT IS REVISION?

Revision requires you to work on the thinking, idea development, organization, and overall content of your writing. Revising might mean that you delete parts of or whole pages, add new paragraphs, make substantial changes to ideas in existing parts of your paper, or completely start over from scratch. None of these changes are unusual or indicate writing deficiency, though you may certainly experience them as difficult and time-consuming. There are no two ways about it: writing is real work. But, it's rewarding, exciting, and always challenging work that can make a difference in how we understand ourselves and others.

Most writers go through several drafts before considering a piece "finished." When you revise, you stand back and reconsider your whole essay, rethinking how its pieces fit together and puzzling through changes that would improve the work overall. In a sense, revision asks that you take a macro and micro view of your work: stepping away from it to get a sense of how your writing is working overall, then examining it closely to make important changes. In addition to improving idea development and organization, we also expect that revisions will reflect careful proofreading and editing.

OUR REVISION POLICY

Our goal is to help you become critical, reflective readers of your writing so that you learn how to engage in meaningful, effective revision on your own. Teacher and peer feedback will help you re-see your essays from a new vantage point. However, revision requires you to do more than make changes based on others' comments—for those comments are always only partial, since readers are not able to identify *everything* that needs to change in order for a draft to improve. ***Your responsibility as the writer is to learn from your readers by taking their feedback seriously and by developing strategies and ideas that are based on your own sense of how to better communicate your message.*** To help you develop into an independent writer who has confidence in your own choices, teachers may stipulate varying revision policies. Nonetheless, despite differing policies, as a program we are unified: revision signifies for us a substantial, thoughtful attempt to rework content and to present a polished, refined draft that reflects your best work.

GUIDELINES
AND FORMS

GUIDELINES
AND FORMS

Overview of Important Dates for Semesters 2012/2013 and 2013/2014

FALL SEMESTER 2012

Classes Begin	Monday, August 27
Holiday: Labor Day	Monday, September 3
Holiday: Veterans Day	Monday, November 12
Holiday: Thanksgiving Weekend	Thursday–Sunday, November 22–25
Classes End	Sunday, December 9
Finals Week	Monday–Saturday, December 10–15

SPRING SEMESTER 2013

Classes Begin	Monday, January 7
Holiday: Dr. Martin Luther King Jr.'s Birthday	Monday, January 21
Spring Break	Monday–Sunday, March 18–24
Classes End	Friday, April 19
Finals Week	Saturday–Thursday, April 20–25

FALL SEMESTER 2013

Classes Begin	Monday, August 26
Holiday: Labor Day	Monday, September 2
Holiday: Veterans Day	Monday, November 11
Holiday: Thanksgiving Weekend	Thursday–Sunday, November 28–December 1
Classes End	Sunday, December 8
Finals Week	Monday–Saturday, December 9–14

SPRING SEMESTER 2014

Classes Begin	Monday, January 6
Holiday: Dr. Martin Luther King Jr.'s Birthday	Monday, January 20
Spring Break	Monday–Sunday, March 17–23
Classes End	Friday, April 18
Finals Week	Saturday–Thursday, April 19–24

Grading Rubric

Departmental policy mandates that students must earn at least a C– or better in 1001 before going on to 2089, the next course in the English Composition sequence. Students receive an A for excellent writing, a B for good writing, and a C for average writing. Students who may need more than a semester to write at a passing level receive the grade of NP (Not Proficient). An NP grade is not punitive in that it does not affect a student's GPA; rather, an NP means students must take the course again to ensure that they have the writing skills they need to succeed in future writing tasks. A grade of F is given in cases of academic dishonesty. (Grades in English 2089—Intermediate Composition, taken the sophomore year, are A through F with no NP.)

AN ESSAY IS EXCELLENT BECAUSE IT

- Meets the guidelines and fulfills expectations of the assignment
- Has a focus that shows originality in thought and approach
- Demonstrates comprehensive understanding of subject matter
- Supports ideas fully with relevant reasons, examples, and details
- Establishes and maintains effective organization
- Reveals an appropriate consideration of audience
- Demonstrates mastery of sentence mechanics

AN ESSAY IS GOOD BECAUSE IT

- Meets the guidelines and fulfills expectations of the assignment
- Has a focus that attempts originality in thought or approach
- Demonstrates good understanding of subject matter
- Supports ideas with sufficient completeness
- Establishes and maintains effective organization
- Reveals an appropriate consideration of audience
- Demonstrates solid understanding of sentence mechanics

AN ESSAY IS AVERAGE BECAUSE IT

- Does not fulfill fully the assignment's guidelines and expectations
- Has a clear focus but sometimes strays from or shifts focus
- Attempts to think beyond the obvious but appears predictable
- Demonstrates critical thought but lacks full engagement with subject matter
- Lacks relevant details and support of ideas
- Shows occasional weaknesses in organization
- Considers audience only generally
- Demonstrates basic understanding of sentence mechanics

AN ESSAY IS BELOW AVERAGE (NP— NOT PROFICIENT) BECAUSE IT

- Fails to fulfill the assignment's guidelines and expectations
- Lacks a focus or shifts focus
- Displays clichéd, lackluster, or overly simplistic writing
- Demonstrates insufficient or cursory engagement with subject matter
- Does not support or develop ideas sufficiently
- Lacks basic organizational structure
- Demonstrates little consideration of audience or is offensive to general readership
- Lacks basic control or understanding of sentence mechanics

This general writing rubric explains some of the evaluation standards instructors apply to essays. However, students should talk with their instructors about how these standards are interpreted in actual writing samples. Keep in mind that evaluations/standards students have had in the past do not necessarily apply here at UC. Students should not expect instructors to grade the way high school teachers did. Rather, they should adapt to the requirements of their present situation and do their best to meet them.

GRADE BREAKDOWN

Grades and quality points are as follows:

Grade	Description	Grade Quality Points	100-point Scale
A	Excellent	4.00	100–95
A–		3.67	94–90
B+	Good	3.33	89–87
B		3.00	86–83
B–		2.67	82–80
C+	Average	2.33	79–77
C		2.00	76–73
C–		1.67	72–70
NP	Not Proficient	N/A	
F	Failure	0.00	
W	Withdrawal (Official)	N/A	
UW	Unofficial Withdrawal	0.00	
X	Unofficial Withdrawal— No participation	0.00	
WX	Official Withdrawal— No participation	N/A	

Sample Essay Evaluation Form

Name: **Date:**

Title:

	Distinctive	Satisfactory	Unsatisfactory	Missing
Focus				
• Focus is relevant to assignment				
• Focus is sustained throughout essay				
Development				
• Ideas thoroughly explained				
• Appropriate tone and consideration of alternative perspectives				
Support				
• Offers a variety of reasons/evidence for opinions				
• Connects evidence/research to focus				
Organization				
• Each paragraph examines one main idea and contains appropriate reasoning for that idea				
• Ideas presented in logical pattern w/ clear transitions				
Mechanics				
• Grammar, spelling, proofreading, sentence clarity				
• Sentence variety and efficiency				

Most of the above categories must be rated satisfactory for the essay to pass.

Responses/Suggestions:

                                                                Yes   No

Meets guidelines and fulfills expectations of the assignment   ☐   ☐

Explanation of Key Terms on the Evaluation Form

FOCUS

The focus of an essay is the thesis/position statement/main claim around which the paper is developed. Say a student decides to write an essay on the topic "spending too much time on the Internet." After giving it more thought, the writer then establishes a focus, e.g., "While the Internet is useful and important to college students, dependence on gaming, social networking, or other Web sites can disrupt a student's daily schedule, impede his communication skills, and even impact his studies." In sum, then, **the focus is the "angle" the writer chooses to take on a particular topic**. Similarly, good or strong writers attempt to present ideas in ways no one else has. An average paper on Internet dependence simply states that it is a problem, while a better paper might argue that students should balance time on e-mail or social networking sites with personal communication, or that schools should provide training on the academic uses of the Internet to help students use the Web for class work. One way, then, to write a good paper is to find a focus that isn't frequently discussed. In short, good writing most often results from thinking about the issue and about how best to express your particular perspective.

DEVELOPMENT

One of the challenges of writing is to think through an idea fully and move beyond simply stating your opinion. Developing an idea often involves asking questions and addressing alternative perspectives. Thinking through an idea during the writing process causes us to question our assumptions and, perhaps, change our minds. Your essays should show that you have considered many aspects of an issue. **Simply stating your opinion and moving on isn't sufficient**. Writers develop their ideas by asking themselves a variety of questions, such as: Who has a stake in this issue and why? Who might have an opinion that differs from mine? How would I address such an opinion? An important

element of development is how well you address alternative perspectives. Good writers are aware of other people's ideas and how they complement or conflict with their own. If such conflict exists, any essay in which the writer rants or insults and dismisses other viewpoints does not show appropriate consideration for readers and will not be persuasive. Successful writers adopt a balanced tone and respectful stance towards their subject matter and readers.

SUPPORT

Remember that every time you write, you try to persuade readers in some fashion. In order to do this successfully, you must show them why they should be persuaded. One effective way is to offer support—**reasons and evidence that corroborate, complicate, and develop your ideas**. Support allows you to offer more than just your opinion. There are many kinds of support, including facts, statistics, survey results, personal anecdotes, hypothetical examples, quotes from interviews, ideas from experts and authorities, and so on.

ORGANIZATION

In paragraphs and in your essay, organization is evident from a clear and logical development necessary and appropriate to the goals of the text. Often, a pattern is evident, but in all cases, a reader is not likely to be confused or lost as happens when one thought seems to lead to an unrelated one. The grading rubric mentions establishing and maintaining effective organization. This means that each sentence should have a main idea, which leads directly into the next sentence. These sentences should combine to form a paragraph with one main purpose. Paragraphs must be linked with clear transition sentences so that your whole paper is unified by a developed, supported focus. Please be aware, however, that this does not happen all at once, and rarely, if ever, happens on a first draft. These links between sentences, paragraphs, and the essay at large often emerge as the piece takes shape.

MECHANICS (SENTENCE COMPLETENESS/VARIETY AND GRAMMAR AND USAGE)

Incomplete or confusing sentences, spelling errors, and grammatical errors interfere with your ability to communicate clearly to your audience, which is a writer's most important task. Consult your English usage handbook or on line resources to learn more about how to avoid and correct errors, and to follow up on feedback your instructor provides.

Class Notes:

Key to Editing Marks

Below are some of the common notations that writing instructors use to alert students to errors. Use the third column to record the page numbers from the *A&B Guide* or other handbook your class is using that refers to the type of error. Use the blank lines at the bottom of the grid to fill in any marks that your professor regularly uses.

Editing Abbreviation	Error	Page Reference *A&B Guide* or English Usage Handbook
Awk	Awkward	
Cap	Capitalization Error	
Cit	Citation Error	
CS	Comma Splice	
DQ	Dropped Quote	
Form	Formatting Error	
Frag	Fragment	
∧	Insert	
Para	Parallelism Error	
Poss	Possessive Error	
P/A	Pronoun/Antecedent Agreement Error	
P	Punctuation Error	
Ref	Faulty, Unclear, or Ambiguous Reference	
R-O	Run-on Sentence	
SP	Spelling	
S/V	Subject/Verb Agreement Error	
WC	Word Choice	

Class Notes:

Plagiarism Explanation and Policy

Plagiarism is using the words or ideas of another without acknowledging and citing the source. The Student Code of Conduct found at http://www.uc.edu/conduct/Code_of_Conduct.html defines "plagiarism" in the following ways:

- Submitting another's published or unpublished work, in whole, in part, or in paraphrase, as one's own without fully and properly crediting the author with footnotes, citations, or bibliographical reference.

- Submitting as one's own original work material obtained from an individual, agency, or the Internet without reference to the person, agency, or web page as the source of the material.

- Submitting as one's own original work material that has been produced through unacknowledged collaboration with others without release in writing from collaborators.

In addition, the English Composition Program considers plagiarism to include the following:

- Submitting as one's own work, without permission to do so, a paper that was co-authored with another student.

- Submitting an essay that you have already received credit for in another class.

Plagiarism can be purposeful, as in the examples above, or accidental. These examples, though perhaps accidental, are also considered plagiarism:

- Failure to cite quotations, paraphrases, summaries, or borrowed ideas.

- Failure to enclose borrowed language in quotation marks.

- Failure to paraphrase appropriately, including changing not only words but also word order.

In the English Composition Program, the penalty for plagiarism, even if it is not intentional, is an automatic grade of F for the course and a letter explaining the offense in your college file. Therefore, if you are unsure about whether or not you have cited all of your work properly, ask your teacher before you submit your essay. The following information will help you learn how to avoid plagiarism. Please also see pages 569–73 in the Allyn & Bacon Guide to Writing.

FREQUENTLY ASKED QUESTIONS ABOUT PLAGIARISM

How will my teacher find out if I plagiarized?
From the first day of the semester to the last, your teacher becomes increasingly familiar with your writing: your particular style, word choices, syntax, critical thinking skills, level of complexity, and ability to organize and develop thoughts. If you submit something that departs in any way from your usual writing style, your teacher will know immediately. **Plagiarism is a serious offense and teachers do investigate their suspicions.** Keep in mind that if you find an essay on the Internet, your teacher can, too. In addition, many teachers require students to submit essays to SafeAssign, an online plagiarism detector program available through Blackboard. Protect yourself by always citing any information from any source you've used to develop your essay.

How do I know when to quote and cite?
Quote and cite anything taken directly from another author. Writers primarily do this when the way in which the phrases are stated is so memorable, or so interesting, or so clearly illustrates a point that paraphrasing the information would not serve the intended purpose. Quotations should be used sparingly and strategically to illustrate and support your ideas, not stand in for them.

How do I know when to cite even if I don't quote?
When the material is not universally known, you need to let the reader know where you discovered this information. If most people already know the information or could find it easily and quickly, you don't need to cite the material.

When in doubt, cite your information but consider the following examples:

George Washington was the first President of the United States.
NO CITATION NEEDED

Some scientists credit the Ponzo illusion, first identified by Mario Ponzo in 1913, to clarify illusions regarding receding parallel lines, to help us understand why the moon sometimes appears larger at the horizon than it does when higher in the sky.
CITATION NEEDED

Happiness is something that many people exhibit by smiling, whereas sadness is often, though not always, reflected in a frown or even tears.
NO CITATION NEEDED

The first astronaut to step foot on the moon was Neil Armstrong.
NO CITATION NEEDED

Sjogren's syndrome is an auto-immune rheumatic disease that often goes undiagnosed. Among other symptoms, it can interrupt the ability of glands to produce moisture, thus causing those afflicted to experience extremely dry membranes, including the inability to produce tears.
CITATION NEEDED

Robert Frost's poem "Birches" reflects the tension between restraint and the unleashing of the imagination.
CITATION if this is the opinion of another author but NO CITATION if this is your own opinion

If you are unsure whether or not to cite information, consult your instructor.

A good rule of thumb is "when in doubt, cite."

WAYS TO AVOID PLAGIARISM

- **Take meticulous notes.** Whenever you conduct research that references the work of others, always be sure to note the following: author's name (spelled correctly); the publication information of the book, magazine, newspaper, Internet site, etc., including the title, publication date, page numbers, and complete Web address.

- **Put direct quotes—anything you copy down word for word—in quotation marks immediately** so you do not confuse them with your own notes. If you take notes carefully and conscientiously throughout your drafting and writing process, you will run less risk of plagiarizing.

- **Be sure you understand your research materials fully.** Without looking at the material, try to put into your own words what you have learned from your research. When you finish, check back to confirm the information. Make sure you didn't unconsciously "borrow" any specific phrases of the author.

- **Use the MLA citation instructions** in the *Allyn & Bacon Guide to Writing* to make sure you have cited everything properly (pp. 576–98).

Publication Consent Form
UNIVERSITY OF CINCINNATI ENGLISH COMPOSITION PROGRAM

Date: _____

Dear Students,

The English Composition Program is always looking for exemplary student writing that we can publish in the next *Student Guide*.

As a result, we are asking for your permission to copy, keep, and perhaps use as examples, the work you have completed this semester. In return for your permission, we promise to remove your name and any other identifying information from the material before it is published, if you wish to remain anonymous.

If you are willing to give this permission, please sign the form at the bottom of this page and return it to your teacher with the relevant essays. There are no negative consequences for not giving permission; we completely understand that your work belongs first and foremost to you.

Thank you for taking this request seriously.

Sincerely,
The English Composition Program

- -

UNIVERSITY OF CINCINNATI ENGLISH COMPOSITION PROGRAM
Publication Consent Form

I _____ (print your name) hereby grant the University of Cincinnati English Composition Program permission to copy and publish—for the purposes of teaching and research—any drafts, revisions, and memos related to my writing.

I understand that my name and any other identifying information will be removed prior to publication, unless I wish to be identified. I **do/do not** (circle one) wish to remain anonymous.

Signature: _____

Date: _____

Teacher's Name: _____

Course/Instructor Evaluation Form

Please answer the following questions honestly and completely about the course you have just taken. Your responses will be used by your instructor to improve the course and by the Composition Program administrators as they evaluate your instructor. Your instructor will not see your evaluation until after the term has ended and grades have been recorded.

There are three parts to this evaluation. Part One asks that you evaluate your work as a student. Part Two asks that you evaluate your instructor's teaching. Part Three asks that you evaluate the course. Your comments are often the most valuable part of these evaluations, so please take your time to add explanations.

PART I. ABOUT YOU, THE STUDENT

Please rate how well you did: (1 is poor, 5 is excellent)

	Poor	Fair	Good	Very Good	Excellent
1. Attending class regularly and on time	1	2	3	4	5
2. Participating in class discussions/activities	1	2	3	4	5
3. Preparing for class (reading, writing, homework)	1	2	3	4	5
4. Willingly revising drafts (on your own or with help)	1	2	3	4	5
5. Accepting criticism from instructor/peers	1	2	3	4	5
6. Improving in reading, writing, thinking over the course of the term	1	2	3	4	5

Please comment on any of the above that you would like to further explain:

PART II. ABOUT YOUR INSTRUCTOR

Please rate how well your instructor did: (1 is poor, 5 is excellent)

	Poor	Fair	Good	Very Good	Excellent
1. Preparing for class	1	2	3	4	5
2. Facilitating class discussions	1	2	3	4	5
3. Encouraging student involvement in class	1	2	3	4	5
4. Clearly explaining assignments	1	2	3	4	5
5. Effectively using Blackboard or other technological resources (skip if not applicable)	1	2	3	4	5
6. Providing useful feedback on assignments	1	2	3	4	5
7. Holding office hours/conferences and communicating	1	2	3	4	5
8. Making class material relevant to writing assignments	1	2	3	4	5
9. Maintaining authority in the classroom	1	2	3	4	5
10. **Overall performance**	1	2	3	4	5

Please comment on any of the above that you would like to further explain:

PART III. ABOUT THE COURSE

On this page, please honestly and thoroughly answer these questions about the course:

1. Specifically, how do you think this course helped you improve as a writer, reader, or researcher?

2. What is your opinion of the readings your class studied this semester? How did they contribute to your understanding of research?

3. Discuss your understanding of the research process and of supporting your points with sources. How did the final research project contribute to this understanding?

4. What helped you best understand rhetoric, analysis, revision, or reflection?

5. Which essay assignment was your favorite and which one posed the biggest challenge for you and why?

6. Were course requirements and expectations clear? Why or why not?

7. Discuss anything else you would like to say about your work, your instructor, or this class.

THE WRITING CENTER

WHAT WE ARE

Our primary purpose is to work with students one-on-one to improve their writing skills so that they can become more competent and self-confident writers. We do not provide editing or proofreading services, though we will be happy to address mechanical and grammatical questions within a tutoring session.

WHERE WE ARE

We are located on the first floor of McMicken Hall in room 149. Please contact us at (513) 556-3912 if you would like to make or change an appointment. You may also stop by the Center to make an appointment. Be aware that appointments fill quickly toward the end of each semester.

WHEN YOU VISIT

Please bring a copy of the assignment, any additional texts pertaining to the assignment, and writing tools. We also encourage you to bring a working draft of the assignment. To ensure that you see a tutor, make your first appointment early in the semester; students who wait until the last minute sometimes find that the schedule is full.

WEB SITE INFORMATION

Visit the English department Web site at http://www.artsci.uc.edu/writingcenter. The website includes contact information, hours of operation, and links to writing resources.

ABOUT OUR STAFF

Our tutoring staff is drawn from a pool of UC writing instructors and advanced students familiar with college-level writing problems and ways to solve them. Our reception staff is drawn from students in the work/study program.

Course Requirements, Goals, and Policies

Instructor:

Office location:

Office hours:

Instructor E-mail:

Instructor Phone:

Course and Section #: 15-ENGL-1001-_____

Course time and location:

Mailbox: McMicken 241 (8 am–5 pm, M–F)

Office phone: English Comp Office: 556-6173 (8 am–5 pm, M–F)

REQUIRED TEXTS

Malek, Joyce, Cynthia Ris, Catherine O'Shea, and Christina LaVecchia, eds. *Student Guide to English Composition 1001, 2012–2014*. Plymouth, MI: Hayden-McNeil, 2012

Ramage, John D., John C. Bean, and June Johnson. *The Allyn & Bacon Guide to Writing*. New York: Pearson-Longman, 2012.

Texts or Reader chosen by your instructor.

COURSE GOALS

- To improve your critical thinking abilities, and therefore your ability to develop complex yet clearly stated written arguments and analyses.
- To introduce you to the composing process and the notion of rhetorical context, and to help you develop strategies for invention and revision.
- To teach you how to develop an appropriate research project, discover and read sources, and write convincingly and persuasively on that subject.
- To encourage you to read and write more critically and carefully now and throughout college and your career.
- To teach you more sophisticated research processes.

COURSE REQUIREMENTS

Attendance
Since writing is an activity, you will learn by doing; much of your time in class will be spent in activities, not lectures. It is important, therefore, that you come to class regularly and that you participate in class activities. If you miss more than one week's worth of classes—for any reason, **including illness**—you may be asked to withdraw. Only religious holidays, military service, and University-sponsored events qualify as "excused" absences. If you miss a class, **it is your responsibility** to find out what you have missed.

Conferences
Your instructor may require conferences during the semester in order to discuss your writing. Even if conferences are not required, most students find that talking with their instructors outside of class can be a helpful supplement to class time. Please check your instructor's office hours or set up an appointment as necessary.

Essays
English 1001 begins by examining how texts are constructed to achieve certain effects. The first assignment introduces you to the concept of rhetoric and the strategy of analysis. The second part of the course focuses on the development of a research project. The project progresses from a series of research steps, resulting in a lengthy argument essay that is then recast into a different genre directed toward a public audience.

Your instructor may ask that you assemble a portfolio so you can see the progress you have made from one assignment to another since each assignment builds on the ones before it, strengthening and developing your skills as a writer.

Peer Review
During the drafting and revising process, your instructor will periodically ask you to exchange copies of your drafts with your peers. To make the most of peer review, you should bring in the strongest draft you can produce in the timeframe and comment thoughtfully and completely on the

work of your peers. After receiving feedback, you will be expected to consider your peers' comments and integrate the changes where necessary. See pp. 445–50 in *A&B* for more information.

Research Steps
Before beginning the research paper, you will complete several shorter assignments designed to address the various phases of the research process. Your teacher will determine the number, type, and due dates of these assignments and explain the necessary length and format for each.

Informal Writing
To help you read carefully and thoughtfully, your teacher may also ask you to respond in a variety of ways to the texts you read for class. In these responses, teachers are primarily concerned with your effort to think seriously and at some length about the assigned topics. Your teacher will explain how these assignments will be evaluated.

COURSE POLICIES AND GRADING

What constitutes a passing essay in 1001?
The evaluation criteria for papers are outlined in the Guidelines section. Essays in English Composition 1001 earn grades in the A, B, or C range. Essays earning less than a C– receive an NP. In order to receive at least a C– an essay must:
- Have a clear and specific focus.
- Show development of ideas with concrete support for claims.
- Exhibit an organizational strategy.
- Meet the length requirement.
- Be properly formatted and sufficiently proofread and edited.

<u>**IMPORTANT:**</u> These are minimum requirements for a C–. To receive a higher mark, you must go above and beyond these requirements. Please see the grading rubric and explanation for further guidance.

Course Grades
In addition to individual essay grades, the following grade breakdown illustrates that your class work and daily assignments impact your final grade in a significant way and should be given the appropriate consideration.

Your instructor will direct you on how to fill in the following grade breakdown:

Texts in Action	_____%
Research Steps	_____%
Researched Argument Essay	_____%
Recast Project	_____%
Informal Writing	_____%
Peer Review Work	_____%
Attendance and Participation	_____%

Possible course grades include A, A–, B+, B, B–, C+, C, C–, NP (Not Proficient), W (Withdrawal), UW (Unofficial Withdrawal), X (Unofficial Withdrawal-No Participation) and WX (Official Withdrawal-No Participation).

Grade Explanation
At the end of the semester, students who have not attained at least a C–, indicating that they are ready for the next course, are assigned the grade of NP, signifying "not proficient." An NP is not a punitive grade (it does not affect your grade point average as an F would); however, it also does not allow you to enroll in English 2089. **If you receive an NP (Not Proficient) as your final course grade, you must retake English Composition 1001.**

For more information on possible course grades like the W, UW, X, and WX, see the UC Registrar's website.

Plagiarism
In the English Composition Program, the penalty for plagiarism, even if it is not intentional, is an **automatic grade of F for the course** and a letter detailing your plagiarism in your college file. Therefore, if you are unsure about whether or not

you have cited all of your work properly, ask your teacher before you submit your essay. The information in the Plagiarism Explanation and Policy will help you learn how to avoid plagiarism. Please also see pp. 569–73 in *A&B*.

FINAL NOTES

1. The *A&S Faculty Handbook* states that students are to behave with civility and appropriate etiquette toward faculty and one another. Noncompliance may lead to disciplinary action as outlined in the *Student Code of Conduct*.

2. Students with disabilities or impairments that will affect their performance or attendance in the course must present their teacher with official documentation from the Disability Services Office during the first two weeks of class so that accommodations can be arranged if necessary.

3. Because teachers make different arrangements regarding grade percentages and revisions, your teacher will explain his or her particular policies in these areas.

4. One of the best ways to help students improve their writing is using examples from class. For this reason, your teacher may be using your writing—without your name attached—in class activities. *If you are strongly opposed to this in general or for specific writing, be sure to mention it to your instructor.*

5. Because technology is not always reliable, and your instructor may ask you to turn in in-process drafts with your essays, make sure you have hard copies of all of the work you do for this class. Keep any work returned with instructor or peer comments—informal writing, peer review drafts, process work, and revisions. Hold on to this work until the end of the semester. Doing so will guard against any unforeseen emergencies (stolen or misplaced essays, faulty computer disks, and viruses).

6. In the university, we regularly communicate using e-mail, Blackboard, and other technological tools. Your instructor will inform you of the preferred method of communication; it is your responsibility to check regularly the preferred tool in order to receive updates and notices about your class.

7. Begin your work early enough to allow plenty of time for revision. Each essay should be revised for content, organization, and grammar. Proofread and edit your work, and consider having at least one other person review it.

8. Because essays in 1001 undergo revision, some instructors don't assign grades to individual drafts, while others assign a grade with the the understanding that the grade is meant as a marker for the work in progress. Any grade an instructor assigns to an individual essay, prior to the final draft of your work, should be used to gauge your progress and need for improvement in the course. This practice gives you the chance to produce the best work you can for your graded evaluation at the end of semester. If you want to know more about how you are doing in the course, we suggest you track the evaluative marks you receive on your informal writing assignments, peer reviews, and class work, which also make up part of your grade. We also suggest that you communicate often with your instructor about your progress.

9. If you stop attending class but do not officially drop the course from your schedule, you will be assigned the grade of UW (Unofficial Withdrawal). This UW factors into your grade point average as 0.0 quality points (the equivalent of an F).

10. Your final grade in English Composition 1001 is determined by several factors, including your final writing, in-class work, informal writing responses, and participation and attendance. If your final work does not pass, you must retake the course. However, because your final

grade takes other activities into consideration, it is possible to have a passing portfolio and still not pass the class because of deficiencies in other areas such as participation and attendance. If you have questions about the Composition Program's minimum standards to pass, see your instructor.

Weekly Schedule of Assignments Due

These dates are meant as guidelines. Consult your instructor for due dates and detailed unit and daily assignments.

Week 1   Microtheme 1: How We Read

Week 2   Submit "Texts in Action" Draft

Week 3   Microtheme 2: Voice

Week 4   Microtheme 6: Genre; Submit Researched Argument Step(s)

Week 5   Submit Researched Argument Step(s) or Microtheme 5: Context

Week 6   Submit Researched Argument Step(s)

Week 7   Submit Researched Argument Proposal

Week 8   Conferences with Instructor (Weeks 7 and 8)

Week 9   Submit Researched Argument Essay Draft

Week 10   Microtheme 4: Style

Week 11

Week 12   Submit or Present Recast Project

Week 13

Week 14   Submit Researched Argument Portfolio, if applicable, and Reflection
Complete Course Evaluations

ENGLISH COMPOSITION 1001

TEXTS IN ACTION

"Not only does text convey information, but it also influences how and what we think. We need to read, then, to understand not only what texts say but also how they say it."

—Richard Bullock,
The Norton Field Guide to Writing (39)

"Democracy cannot succeed unless those who express their choice are prepared to choose wisely. The real safeguard of democracy, therefore, is education."

—Franklin D. Roosevelt,
quoted in *Composing a Civic Life* (xix)

Texts In Action

■ KEY ASSIGNMENT

Write an essay in which you analyze the relationship between persuasion and action, behavior, and/or beliefs.

■ FORMAT

1200–1550 words or 4–5 pages, MLA format

ASSIGNMENT OPTIONS

- Working with a written text that clearly aims to persuade, analyze and assess its effectiveness within a specific context. What strategies are used to influence the attitudes, actions, or beliefs of a particular audience? What's the original purpose and context of the text? If it's dated, how has the passage of time affected the text's persuasiveness or altered its original purpose?

- Analyze a print or visual text by focusing on how its genre is central to its persuasive power. Your analysis should examine how the chosen genre interacts with the kind of action, behavior, and/or belief that the text encourages. In other words, ask yourself what difference the genre makes to the text's persuasiveness; what if it were written in a different genre?

- Examine no more than two visual texts that aim to persuade viewers to act or behave in a particular way and analyze how the texts define *meaningful action*.

- Analyze one section of the UC website with the goal of understanding how the university brands itself. Think about how the site uses language, images, testimonials, data, and other forms of evidence to influence beliefs and actions.

- Study the link between action and writing by analyzing a series of public texts with the intent of developing a better understanding of how audiences are envisioned in these texts and how they are encouraged or expected to act in response to a particular issue. Possible sites of analysis include locally relevant texts (*The News Record*; The Hamilton County Park District website; *Cincinnati Magazine*, etc.) or national/international ones like *The New York Times*, the It Gets Better Project, *Slate Magazine*, and so forth.

A&B QUICK REFERENCES: ANALYSIS

- Concept 3: Good writers think rhetorically about purpose, audience, and genre, pp. 15–23
- Concept 8: Messages persuade through their angle of vision, pp. 52–57
- Concept 9: Messages appeal through appeals to logos, ethos, and pathos, p. 58

- Interview editors or writers of a local organization (on or off campus) to find out how they use persuasion explicitly to incite action. In addition, collect examples of written or visual material related to that organization. Finally, write a report that incorporates your findings from the interviews and analyzes how the examples address the purpose and function of the organization.

- Other options as determined by your instructor.

ASSIGNMENT GOALS

- To recognize the power of language to move people to action, whether action takes a public or private form.
- To understand which rhetorical strategies are frequently used to motivate people to act.
- To identify the powerful relationships between communication, action, and democracy.
- To develop strategies for generating writing that inspires action.
- To learn about rhetoric and rhetorical strategies and to apply that knowledge in writing.
- To recognize rhetorical strategies as purposeful, deliberate choices.
- To understand how writers craft arguments to persuade different audiences.
- To develop and sustain an idea through a well-organized, thesis-driven essay, supported with relevant evidence and examples.
- To demonstrate reasonable sentence-level control, including syntax and grammar competency, and to cite source material using MLA conventions.

DISCUSSION OF ASSIGNMENT

In this unit your aim is to understand how language influences beliefs, attitudes, and/or behaviors. This assignment will give you a better appreciation for, and a heightened awareness of, how people use rhetoric for persuasive purposes—in the process, you'll no doubt learn how you might do the same.

This assignment asks you to reckon with the idea that every text is shaped in particular and intentional ways to have certain effects on readers or viewers. Think of your analysis as a behind-the-scenes exploration of a writer's rhetorical choices. With this goal in mind, you'll want to focus on how the message—especially injunctions to feel, believe, or act in certain ways—is composed and delivered for specific audiences at certain moments in time.

A & B QUICK
REFERENCES:

FOCUS

- Question—Asking Strategies for Writing a Rhetorical Critique, pp. 105–06
- Concept 7: Thesis statements in closed-form prose are supported hierarchically with points and particulars, pp. 46–49
- Skill 17.3: Plan and visualize your structure, pp. 459–64

SOME QUESTIONS TO CONSIDER

- What kinds of conversations and concerns are already circulating in the text's targeted audience?
- How does the text fit into those conversations? How does it echo or challenge a community's values?
- How does the author develop authority with the audience?
- Who, or which communities, are the audiences for this text—who was meant to read it? What specific features of the text help you figure this out?
- What is the author's purpose? What is the desired outcome or result?
- What kinds of assumptions does the writer make about his/her audience's values, identities, community memberships? Is he or she successful at addressing them?

TIPS

You will need to back up your analysis with specific evidence, including, for instance, discussion of tone, use of sources, rhetorical appeals, and use of examples and evidence. You might also consider how the author went about constructing the text. What are the advantages and drawbacks of her or his methods? What might be the biggest weakness?

PURPOSE WITHIN 1001 CURRICULUM

This assignment asks you to examine how and why a text is put together in a certain way and what effects its rhetorical components have on an audience. By understanding and employing rhetoric, you will be well equipped to engage with texts of all sorts, both within and beyond college. Likewise, analysis is an important skill central to a broad range of writing and thinking tasks that you'll encounter in your education and in your career.

This assignment, like most others in the composition sequence, begins from the premise that rhetoric is the framework for understanding how and why people communicate, and analysis is a primary tool by which we come to such an understanding.

ACTIVITIES

In each Unit, you'll find activities to help you compose, revise, and reflect upon the essay assigned. In addition to the activities outlined, please also consult the *A&B Guide* for many productive approaches to writing, revising, and reflecting. In particular, we recommend that you consult the following chapters in Part 3: A Guide to Composing and Revising: Chapter 16, Writing as a Problem-Solving Process, and Chapter 18, Composing and Revising Closed-Form Prose. Additionally, in Part 5, see Chapter 24: Portfolio and Reflective Essays, and in Part 6: A Guide to Editing, see Chapter 1: Improving Your Editing Skills, Chapter 2: Understanding Sentence Structure, and Chapter 5: Editing for Style.

In addition, peer review prompts and suggestions are available throughout the book.

Composing

a. Use your confusion. In other words, identify the passages in the text that seem unusual to you. Rather than letting yourself be drawn to the spots in the text that you recognize and understand, seek out unfamiliar words, phrases, and ideas. Look for instances in the text where the tone, voice, or attitude seems unconventional or even strange. Chances are, these moments in the text signal deliberate rhetorical choices the author is making to affect the audience's response to the text. Make a list of these aspects and use them as a resource when formulating your analysis.

b. One way to analyze the meaning and function of a written work is to use a strategy called "Descriptive Outline" or "Says/Does." To perform a "Says/Does" analysis, read through an essay, writing a "says" statement and a "does" statement for each paragraph (either in the margin or in the table provided on the following page). A "says" statement is a **one-sentence summary** (not a phrase or a few words) of the paragraph's main idea. It summarizes the meaning or message of a paragraph. A "does" statement **describes the function of a paragraph**—what it does. "Does" statements use words like "introduces," "provides evidence," "presents opposing viewpoint," "accommodates opposing viewpoint," "refutes," etc. See the example on page 33.

In addition to using "Says/Does" to get at the meaning and function of paragraphs in a reading, you can also apply "says/does" to your own writing to examine it for organization and development of your ideas.

Revising

Copy and paste your introduction and conclusion in a new document and read through them. What is repeated, and what's useful or advantageous about these repetitions? Do the two together show that you traveled somewhere in the course of your paper? In other words, do you get to any new insights or realizations by the end of the paper, or do you echo your beginning points? Once you've considered these questions, make any necessary changes.

You could do a similar exercise with a partner in class. Trade papers, reading each others' intros and conclusions, and then offer feedback on what you can infer about the paper as a whole. Comment on what's effective or ineffective in the intros and conclusions.

 For more on intros and conclusions, see *A&B* pp. 466–68 and 492–93.

Reflecting

a. Reread your draft with these questions in mind: What one aspect about this paper was the most challenging? How did you approach that challenge? Then write an informal reflection in which you answer these questions in relaxed, conversational language. Don't consult your paper as you write; strive, instead, to put your ideas into everyday language, as if you're describing your paper-writing process to a friend. Use your reflective insights for revision. Having identified and articulated the part of the assignment that gave you the most trouble, you might find it far less daunting now.

b. Write a 1–2 page reflection about your writing process for this essay. How was the experience of writing it similar to other papers you've written? How was it different? Did you try any new drafting strategies that either succeeded or failed? Do you see yourself falling back on any bad habits or still searching for ways to make specific improvements?

Read A.J. Chavez's essay "The Case for (Gay) Marriage," in *A&B* pp. 372–6, and construct "Says/Does" statements for each paragraph. The first four paragraphs (¶) have been done for you.

	SAYS	DOES
¶1	Basic rights taken for granted by married couples are denied to same-sex couples.	This paragraph introduces the topic with a compelling scenario to get readers' attention and arouse sympathy for the claim.
¶2	Gay marriage should be legalized nation-wide—at the federal level—for social, political, and economic reasons.	This paragraph provides the essay's claim and outlines reasons for supporting the claim.
¶3	Many arguments against gay marriage exist ranging from definitions of marriage: objections on religious and moral grounds, to beliefs that protection for gay couples already exists, to fears that extending rights to gay couples will lead to "more radical unions," and rejection of marriage from gay couples themselves.	This paragraph outlines several objections to the claim.
¶4	Gay marriage must be recognized at the federal level to guarantee equal rights to gay couples and to prevent exclusions from state-to-state that civil unions would allow.	This paragraph addresses political objections and details reasons to support the claim.
¶5		
¶6		
¶7		
¶8		

Unit Two

MAKING
A CLAIM

Introduction
Part One: Research Steps
Part Two: Researched Argument

Making a Claim

This unit has **two parts**: 1) a series of shorter explorations, or research steps, designed to prepare you to write a research-based argument essay, and 2) the researched argument essay itself.

Because engaging in professional discussion is central to success in any field, you need to learn how to position yourself in relation to relevant and timely conversations and contribute your own informed perspective to them.

The research steps in **Part One** will help you explore, expand, reconsider, and reflect on the various conversations that surround current and compelling questions or problems. We hope these exploratory assignments will convince you of the rewards and challenges entailed in self-directed, complex writing projects.

Part Two, the researched argument essay, will bring together many of the skills you've been developing throughout the course—close reading, balancing and documenting sources, developing an arguable thesis or claim, and choosing appropriate language and rhetorical strategies to make your case.

Part One: Research Steps UNIT 2

■ KEY ASSIGNMENT

Develop a guiding research question or set of questions for the researched argument in Unit 2.

UNIT TWO: PART ONE DESCRIPTION

Your task for the first part of this unit is to explore, discover, and engage with an academic, cultural, or professional debate through one or more research and writing steps selected by your instructor. These steps are designed to guide you towards developing a clear and focused research question and hypothesis for your final researched argument paper in part two of this unit. This is a crucial component in the development of an effective argument that has relevance both to you and your readers. While we all know how to ask questions, many of us could use practice *crafting* questions that lead to worthwhile research projects—projects that uncover and persuasively present valuable, informed insights about a given topic. The purpose of this unit is to provide you with opportunities to get that practice.

STEPS

A. **Understanding and Using Sources for Discovery**
   Finding and Evaluating Library Sources
   Evaluating Internet Sources
   Developing and Annotated Bibliography

B. **Determining a Research Topic**

C. **Entering the Conversation**
   Creating a Dialogue
   Exploring Your Topic
   Conducting an Interview
   Constructing a Questionnaire

D. **Determining a Focus and Mapping a Plan**
   Moving from Topic to Plan
   Mapping Your Ideas
   Considering a Thesis
   Outlining an Argument
   Writing a Hypothesis

E. **Proposing Your Research Project**
   Drafting Your Research Proposal
   Presenting Your Research Proposal

GOALS

- To learn how to ask researchable questions that have complexity and that engage you as a thinker, reader, and writer.
- To emphasize discovery as generative for writing an effective, informed, and timely researched argument.
- To prepare you for the thinking, writing, and researching necessary to write a re-searched argument.
- To familiarize you with research conventions and methods for finding relevant source material.
- To expose you to multiple research genres (i.e., annotated bibliography, proposal, pre-sentation) and their differing purposes and rationales.
- To learn how to initiate, sustain, and complete an extended research project.

PURPOSE WITHIN 1001 CURRICULUM

This part of Unit 2 provides the framework for an in-depth, research-based argument. Be-cause engaging in professional discussion is central to success in any field, you need to learn how to position yourself in relation to disciplinary conversations and contribute your own informed perspective to them. The projects in this part of the unit are a series of shorter explorations designed to prepare you to write successfully the culminating essay in the first-year composition series. We also hope these exploratory assignments will convince you of the rewards and challenges entailed in self-directed, complex writing projects.

RESEARCH STEPS DESCRIPTIONS
A. UNDERSTANDING AND USING SOURCES FOR DISCOVERY

Finding and Evaluating Library Sources
1. Locate three sources on a topic idea: 1) an academic or professional journal article, 2) a mainstream magazine article, and 3) a newspaper article. Print/copy each article in its entirety.
2. Write a brief summary of each source. What are the main points? (Do not simply copy the abstract; write your own summary.)
3. Write a paragraph evaluating the sources. Include your opinions on the source's publica-tion date, the author's credibility or reputation, the type of source, possible bias in the source, and readability.
4. Write an MLA works cited entry for each source.
5. Attach a copy of each source.

   For more information on finding and evaluating library sources, see Part 4 in *A&B*.

Evaluating Internet Sources
1. Using any internet search engine, search the key words of a topic idea.
2. Look at six sites that you would consider valid for your research topic. Do not just choose the first six you find. Look closely at the URL, the description of the site, the search word

combinations that come up in the site, and of course the title of the site.

3. Record the correct MLA citation for each site.

4. Look closely at what organization built the site, what the main purpose of the site is (general information, article, FAQs), and the rhetorical techniques used in the presentation of the site (layout, format, information links).

5. Write a short paragraph (three or four sentences) on whether or not this site would be helpful to your research project.

 For more information on finding and evaluating internet sources, see *A&B* pp. 532–35 and 544–50.

Developing an Annotated Bibliography

One way to discover possible research topics is to do some initial research on issues, topics, or ideas that interest you. Find a few reputable sources on each topic. Compose an annotated bibliography that details the issues at stake within each topic. Each entry should contain: 1) a properly formatted citation for the source, and 2) a paragraph or two in which you explain the main ideas of the source, how it relates to the topic, and what ideas for your own project you had after reading it.

 For more information on citing and creating an effective annotated bibliography, see *A&B* pp. 164–67 and 576–89.

B. DETERMINING A RESEARCH PROJECT

Choosing a research topic can be a very difficult decision. Your topic must be arguable, it must have scholarly value, it must be broad enough for a balanced discussion, and it should allow you to enter and add to the conversation. Because it needs to be manageable, it should also be narrow enough for a detailed discussion of relevant issues in the topic.

List three issues or topics that you are interested in exploring further and answer the following questions about each issue:

- What do you "know" and "believe" about this issue?
- How did you develop understanding of the issue?
- What are the central questions that need to be addressed in relation to this issue?
- What are (or do you suppose) would be at least two important objections to your stance on the issue?

Once you have the essentials of each issue you are considering for your topic, you can begin to narrow your ideas down to one issue. Things to think about are your interest in this topic, your ability to fully research the topic, and whether or not the issue is debatable.

 For more information on developing a focused research question, see *A&B* pp. 518–20.

C. ENTERING THE CONVERSATION

Creating a Dialogue

Since the research process is social—a process where people create a conversation of ideas, facts, and theories surrounding a topic—it is important for you to understand that conversation and contribute to it yourself. By creating a conversation among your sources and yourself, you will be better able to visualize the scope of your subject and how each of your sources contributes to it. This process will help you discover how you might use each source in your own project and how your own ideas and argument fit into the larger discussion.

For this project, you will create a fictionalized conversation between three or four of your sources with you as the moderator. Imagine that you are writing out a transcript of a panel discussion. You will include actual quotes and paraphrases from the sources as well as completely fictionalized statements that truly represent the sources' opinions and ideas. As the moderator of the panel, you should pose questions to your sources and respond to their "responses." Try to choose sources that have different perspectives on your topic.

   For more information on accurately representing sources, see *A&B* pp. 558–65.

Exploring Your Topic

After you've completed projects in Part A that helped you to discover a topic and find sources related to it, you'll want to "enter the conversation" about it by expressing your perspective. You might not yet know what your perspective is or what you can add. One way to approach this problem is through brief pieces of informal writing that allow you to explore what you think about your subject and why you're interested in it.

Here are a few suggestions that can help you add your voice and perspective to the conversation about your topic:

- **Metaphor or Extended Analogy**
  Use templates to recharge your thinking about your topic and take it in surprising directions such as "This topic is like_____," or "This topic is like_____, but it is also like (or unlike)_____," or "If this topic were a _____, it would be like this_____." Extend your metaphor or analogy into at least a page of single-spaced writing.

  Examples: "Writing is like walking through tall grass." "Writing is like walking through tall grass, but it is also like cutting a new path." "If writing were like driving a car, I'd have a thousand crashes by now."

- **Thought Letter**
  Write a letter or e-mail message about your topic to a friend or family member, explaining to them what interests you about it and what questions or problems it poses for you.

- **"Cubing"**
  Approach your topic by posing answers to six questions representing sides of a cube: Who, what, where, when, how, why.

- **What Else?**
  Draft a list of what you still don't know about your topic. How would you find this information?

Conducting an Interview

The point of this activity is to interview someone who can address your questions with some expertise. Find a professional who specializes or possesses noteworthy experience in your topic or area of interest. Once you identify several possible candidates, contact them via email, phone, or in person. Be sure to explain the purpose of the interview and to describe your research project clearly and succinctly. Then ask the candidate if he/she would be willing to meet with you, and, if so, what dates/times work best. You should indicate the date by when you will need to conduct the interview, preferably well in advance of the assignment deadline. You might also ask if you can record the interview. Keep in mind that interview can fall through, so it is wise to have a back-up plan.

 For more information on conducting an interview, see *A&B* pp. 207–10

Constructing a Questionnaire

Develop a set of questions related to your research project that will provide you with relevant information. Following *Allyn & Bacon's* advice, "imagine respondents with only limited patience and time. Keep your questionnaire clear, easy to complete, and as short as possible, taking care to avoid ambiguous sentences" (210).

 For more information on constructing a questionnaire, see *A&B* pp. 210–13.

D. DETERMINING A FOCUS AND MAPPING A PLAN

Moving From Topic to Plan

In order to avoid what *Allyn & Bacon's* editors call a "data dump," you will need to develop a claim about your topic. After doing some initial research on your topic, write a three-paragraph exploration of a way to narrow your focus and develop a possible claim.

In the first paragraph, introduce your research paper topic and describe what you think the main focus of the project might be. Include a working thesis in this paragraph, which you can revise later. In the second paragraph, discuss what others have said about this issue, referencing your sources specifically and anticipating additional research you may have to do. In the third paragraph, speculate on what obstacles you foresee in this project and/or what you anticipate to be the most difficult part of the assignment.

Mapping Your Ideas

After you have gathered your research, taken purposeful notes, and considered the issue thoroughly, you may find that you are overwhelmed with information. By putting that information in a visual form, you may discover connections and patterns that can be used to structure your paper.

First, take ten to fifteen minutes and list everything you can about your topic. Don't worry about whether it is relevant; if you think it, write it. Now, using your topic as a focal point, map out items from your list, drawing connections between items. You can use different colors or shapes to group and categorize items as well.

 For more information on how to create a visual map, see *A&B* pp. 31–32 and 461–64.

Considering a Thesis

In order to work on developing a strong thesis, write what you believe your reader thinks about your topic before reading your essay and then how your reader will think differently about your topic after reading your essay. Now turn to *A&B* pp. 37–42 in order to review and implement strategies by which you can change a reader's view of your topic, develop a thesis statement with tension, and surprise a reader. Draft several versions of your thesis statement with these strategies in mind and exchange with a partner for discussion and feedback.

Outlining an Argument

Drawing on the material you have generated for your topic, research question, and source material, start to categorize what material will be included in which sections of the essay and sketch a possible order for those sections. It may help to have your thesis statement (or a draft of it) written out at the top of the page so that you can be sure all your points relate directly back to your thesis. Your outline may be formatted in a number of ways, but it should provide a blueprint of your argument that you can use to draft your paper.

 For more information on how to create an outline, see *A&B* p. 458–62.

Writing a Hypothesis

Once you have a specific issue that you are interested in pursuing, you should consider what your position is. To do this, you will need to determine your role as a researcher and what you want to accomplish. List two or three possible roles. What questions would each type of researcher ask? List two for each. Now, for each of those questions, formulate a considered answer. You now have a number of possible claims. Look over these hypotheses to see which one you wish to pursue further.

 For more information on researching roles, see *A&B* pp. 518–21.

E. PROPOSING YOUR RESEARCH PROJECT

Drafting Your Research Proposal

After you have explored your topic by writing about it and conducting some preliminary research, gather your ideas in the form of a proposal that you will submit to your instructor. The type of proposal you'll write for this research step differs from those described in *A&B* Chapter 15, which propose solutions to problems. Instead, we're asking for one that more closely resembles those submitted in response to calls for papers written for academic journals or conferences. For this type of proposal, your readers assume that through the preliminary research you've been conducting, you have developed a position on a topic or issue that you wish to explore further, and that will, in this case, result in an extended essay.

Your proposal should include:

- a **working title**
- the **research question** you've been exploring
- your **claim** or thesis supported by **reasons for your position**
- a **discussion section** that provides a brief background of the issue, outlines the viewpoints you'll discuss, and states the evidence or sources you'll use
- a **research schedule**
- a **biographical note** that explains your interest and background and expertise with regard to the topic

 For more information on research questions and approaches, see *A&B* pp. 518–21.

Presenting Your Research Proposal

This assignment requires you to create a brief presentation of your researched argument essay. Your goal is to identify for your audience the central question(s) that will guide your essay. In addition, your presentation should make clear what's at stake in your argument by explaining how a select number of experts address the question(s) you pose. Be sure to include your own preliminary response to your question as well. Your teacher will determine the format (i.e., oral, visual, or both), length, and number of sources required for the presentation.

 For more information on how to create an effective oral presentation, see *A&B* pp. 415–21.

Part Two: Researched Argument

■ KEY ASSIGNMENT

Write a researched argument that evolves from the question(s) you developed in the first part of the unit. Your goal is to shape the question(s) into an argument with a clearly identified purpose and audience. Convince your audience of the merit of your position by using evidence from an appropriately diverse and relevant set of sources.

■ FORMAT

6–8 pages or 2100–2800 words, MLA format

ASSIGNMENT DESCRIPTION

Research writing is very demanding—it involves close reading, rhetorical analysis, synthesis of conflicting and complementary ideas, careful representation of others' words, and the development of your own position and voice in a way that is distinct from, though influenced by, the source material you use to support your position.

In addition, we believe the foundation of strong research writing makes all the difference: learning how to ask researchable questions that are complex (i.e., not sufficiently answered by "yes" or "no"), compelling, and motivated by a genuine desire to know something. Research writing, in other words, is not a "data dump" or a simple transcription of what others have said about your topic. It is an act of inquiry motivated by a question or set of questions that have some tension.

Crafting a strong argument calls on you to identify arguable issues, take a position, and consider and respond to other perspectives that might conflict with or challenge your own. It involves seeing argument as active, not as a pro/con debate. We encourage you to approach your researched argument with this view of research writing in mind; doing so, we hope, will make the writing meaningful and worthwhile to you personally, in addition to fulfilling the assignment.

A & B QUICK REFERENCES:

CONDUCTING RESEARCH

- Skill 21.2: Know when and how to use summary, paraphrase, and quotation, pp. 558–61
- Skill 21.3: Use attributive tags to distinguish your ideas from a source, pp. 561–65
- Skill 21.4: Punctuate quotations correctly, pp. 565–69
- Skill 21.5: Avoid plagiarism by following academic conventions for ethical use of sources, pp. 569–73
- Chapter 22: Citing and Documenting Sources, pp. 574–605
- Collecting Data through Observations, Interviews, or Questionnaires, pp. 207–13

ASSIGNMENT GOALS

- To participate in and contribute to the larger conversation around your topic.
- To understand research as inquiry-based, that is, as that which evolves from informed, well-crafted questions.
- To understand that argument is rhetorically complex and not reducible to pro/con positions.
- To articulate a claim and support it with relevant, timely evidence.
- To acknowledge counter-claims while maintaining control of your argument.
- To select and balance a variety of sources that relate to your argument.
- To integrate source material by quoting, paraphrasing, and summarizing.
- To develop and sustain an idea through a well-organized, thesis-driven essay supported with relevant evidence and examples.
- To demonstrate reasonable sentence-level control, including syntax and grammar competency, and to cite source material using MLA conventions.

ASSIGNMENT PURPOSE WITHIN THE 1001 CURRICULUM

This essay involves close reading, summary, rhetorical analysis, and synthesis. In addition, it asks that you sustain and develop an extended persuasive argument using research in an appropriate and convincing way. This assignment puts particular emphasis on your ability to articulate a strong question that you develop and refine through drafting and revision. We include a researched argument in first-year composition because it prepares you to understand and respond to debatable issues in a range of reading, writing, and thinking situations.

A&B QUICK REFERENCES: CONSTRUCTING AN ARGUMENT

- Concept 5: A strong thesis statement surprises readers with something new or challenging, pp. 37–42
- Concept 6: In closed-form prose, a typical introduction starts with the problem, not the thesis, pp. 42–46
- Concept 7: Thesis statements in closed-form prose are supported hierarchically with points and particulars, pp. 46–49
- Skill 21.1: Let your own argument determine your use of sources, pp. 555–57
- Chapter 13: Writing a Classical Argument, pp. 331–77

REVISING ACTIVITY

adds
speculates
concludes
sees
explains
asks
refuses
contends
illustrates
claims
reports
denies
warns
maintains
concedes
complains
emphasizes
argues
points out
considers
notes
holds
believes
relates
defends
thinks
insists
compares
suggests
disputes
agrees
observes
condemns
shows
finds
asserts
rejects
declares
reveals
implies
comments
responds
disagrees
writes

A. DESCRIPTIVE VERBS AND ATTRIBUTIVE TAGS

When introducing quotations and/or paraphrased ideas in an attributive tag, it can be tempting to repeat the standard "says" or "states" for every source. But carefully considered verbs can have great effect; not only will your sentences have more energy and variety, but you can also affect your readers' perspective on the incorporated source material.

1. Read through a draft of your researched argument essay and locate a quote or paraphrase introduced with a simple "says" or "states." Choose a more fitting descriptive verb from the list provided. Write the revised sentence(s) below:

2. How might this small verb change help your reader see or understand the source material differently?

3. Using *A&B* pp. 561–65, decide what other information would be helpful to the reader and add it to the sentence(s) above.

4. How do these additions help your reader see or understand the quoted material differently?

5. Finally, in your draft, inspect each quote or paraphrase. Write or revise attributive tags with descriptive verbs for each. Be sure that any quoted sentence isn't standing alone (this is called a dropped quote). Also, be sure that after each quote/paraphrase, you have explained how it relates to your point as this is an important connection to make clear to your reader. The following is an easy formula to keep in mind:

> Intro source with attributive tag and descriptive verb
> +
> "quotation" or paraphrase
> +
> How the quote/paraphrase relates to your point
> =
> a well-incorporated source

B. OUTLINING YOUR PAPER

Reread your paper and write an outline of it. Your outline should identify the main idea that organizes each paragraph as well as the supporting information (i.e., factual data, anecdotal evidence, interpretation, summary, paraphrase, quotation, etc.). Once you've written your outline, look it over with an eye toward jumps in logic, confusing organization, unsupported claims, and less-than-relevant support of your main ideas. Write a brief one-page response to your outline: What did you learn through outlining? What will you take from this exercise and apply to your next draft?

 For more information, see *A&B* pp. 459–64.

Reflecting

Before finalizing your draft, write a paragraph or two in which you describe your essay at the current moment. Imagine yourself representing your essay to someone who hasn't read it as you define your aim and comment on the present strengths and weaknesses. Use this informal piece as a guide for revising before you submit your final draft.

Unit Three

ENGLISH
COMPOSITION 1001

RECASTING
FOR A PUBLIC
AUDIENCE

Recasting for a Public Audience UNIT 3

■ KEY ASSIGNMENT

Recast your researched argument for a different audience and purpose. Accompany your recast with a rationale that explains the choices you made in creating and composing your recast project.

■ FORMAT

Determined by the option chosen and your instructor's requirements.

ASSIGNMENT DESCRIPTION

Now that you have researched your topic and written a formal, academic argument essay, this assignment provides an opportunity to present your researched argument in a new or different way: to recast it, perhaps as a visual argument, an editorial, or some other public form. We call this work a "recast" because it retains the imprint or key elements of your original essay while changing its shape and focus.

The goals of this project are to share your work with more people than your instructor and to be aware of the various decisions that you need to make when working with different audiences and different media. You or your instructor will choose a group as the target audience of your text. The audience might be more generally defined (the class, other college students, older adults, etc.) or more narrowly defined (female UC undergraduates, senior citizens living in rural areas of Ohio, high school seniors considering

> **A & B QUICK REFERENCES:**
>
> - Messages persuade through appeals to logos, ethos, and pathos, pp. 58–59
> - Appealing to *Ethos* and *Pathos*, pp. 348–50
> - Chapter 13: Writing a Classical Argument, pp. 331–77

colleges, etc.) determined by the message you wish to convey. Each of the recast projects should be accompanied by a two-to-three page written rationale that discusses your project's purpose, the form (medium or genre) of your project, the audience your recast project is directed toward, and the rhetorical choices you made in writing or creating your recast. **In effect, your rationale should make an argument about your project's purpose and effectiveness.**

Option 1: Article for publication in a public forum

Recast your argument into an editorial or article for publication in a print-based or web-based forum. This project calls on you to capture your argument in a briefer form directed toward a specific audience. You will need to consider the submission requirements of the publication, its readership, and focus. Your submission should be relevant, current, and compelling to your publication's readers. Accompany your article with a two-to-three page rationale that discusses your audience, the purpose of your editorial or article, the conventions of the genre and how you met them, and the rhetorical choices you made.

Option 2: Advocacy Text

Recast your essay as a public service poster, advocacy ad, website, or pamphlet. Create an advocacy ad, poster, website, or pamphlet that recasts the issue argued in your research essay as a public problem that calls for action and support. This project calls on you to capture your argument in a highly condensed form, while making it visually clear and memorable. You will need to consider all the features of visual arguments—type sizes and fonts, layout, color, and images and graphics—to grab the attention of your audience, construct a compelling sketch of the problem, and inform your audience what course of action you want them to take. (See *A&B* p. 412.)

Accompany your project with a two-to-three-page rationale that describes and explains the choices you made in designing it. Your rationale should discuss your audience, the goal or purpose of your project, the conventions of the genre and how you met them, and the rhetorical choices you made in its composition.

Option 3: Proposal Speech with Visual Aids

Recast your researched argument essay as a prepared speech of approximately five to eight minutes supported with visual aids. Your speech should represent the issue argued in your research essay as a problem, propose a solution, justify the solution with reasons and evidence, and defend it against objections or alternative solutions. As you deliver your speech, use appropriate visual aids to give presence to the problem, highlight points, provide memorable data or evidence, or otherwise enhance appeals to *logos*, *ethos*, and *pathos*. (See A&B p. 414.) Accompany your speech with a two-to-three page rationale that discusses your audience, the purpose of your speech, and the rhetorical choices you made in your delivery.

Option 4

Other options as determined by your instructor.

A & B QUICK REFERENCES:

- Visual Rhetoric, pp. 59–60
- Proposals as Visual Arguments and PowerPoint Presentations, pp. 406–11
- Advocacy Ad or Poster, pp. 412–14
- Using Evidence Effectively, pp. 339–42
- Developing, Shaping, and Outlining Your Proposal Speech, pp. 414–22

ASSIGNMENT GOALS

- To understand that researched writing can be reworked for different audiences.
- To explore different genres as possibilities for your writing.
- To consider how the needs of a public audience affect choices in communicating your message.
- To demonstrate how to represent yourself through your work to a public audience.
- To demonstrate how to present your purpose and argument to best suit your audience's needs and expectations.

ASSIGNMENT PURPOSE WITHIN THE 1001 CURRICULUM

This assignment asks that you reconsider the purpose of your project, its goals and focus, and the needs and expectations of your audience. Because this assignment is meant for an audience different than the one you directed your research essay toward, it gives you an opportunity to refocus your research with a new purpose, audience, and context in mind. It prepares you to do the kinds of thinking and writing required to successfully communicate a message to various discourse communities, whether the community is formal or informal, familiar or unfamiliar, academic or nonacademic. Finally, it asks you to work with genre, one of the areas emphasized in Intermediate Composition, the final course in the English Composition sequence.

ACTIVITIES

Composing

For this activity, set a timer for ten minutes and write *about* your argument essay. Let your thoughts move to what you found most interesting, most generative, or most unsettled in your work. The goal of freewriting like this is not to write fast, but to write continuously without stopping until the timer goes off. Try to ignore errors and avoid stopping and correcting your work as you write. After you've written for ten minutes, look back at what you wrote and pick out a word, phrase, or idea that stands out to you and that you wish to explore in another round of ten-minute writing. Write the word, phrase, or idea at the top of another page and write about it for ten minutes, letting the writing take you where it will. Aim for three rounds of writing, repeating the process each time.

Reflecting

Imagine an ideal reader or audience for your recast project. What interests your reader? What is your reader most passionate about? What activities, groups, or organizations is your reader involved in? What would your reader find most intriguing about your project? What do you expect that your reader will do or think after reading or viewing your project? What would your reader want to talk to you about after reading or viewing your project? What would you like to tell your reader about your project?

ENGLISH
COMPOSITION 1001

REFLECTING
ON YOUR
WORK

Reflecting on Your Work

Write a reflective essay, or an analysis of your writing experiences, that grows out of the writing and revising you did this semester, with particular emphasis on how you hope to transfer what you learned in this class to other writing situations.

■ FORMAT

1–2 pages

ASSIGNMENT DESCRIPTION

During the course of the semester as you have been drafting, researching, and revising, you have also been writing short, reflective pieces (i.e., in-class freewriting, process writes, quick writes, directed reflections, journal entries, etc.) about your rhetorical choices and about your experience with argument-based writing. These brief reflections allowed you to pause and consider your work as it was occurring so that you could become more aware of your learning and composing processes.

This final reflective assignment calls for you to examine more comprehensively the work you have done this term by writing about the rhetorical choices you made in composing the two major assignments: the researched argument essay and the recast essay. The assignment asks that you analyze what your work reveals about yourself as a writer so that you can "apply that learning to future writing situations" (*A&B* p. 623).

> **A & B QUICK REFERENCES:**
>
> - Chapter 24: Portfolios and Reflective Essays
> - Understanding Reflective Writing, pp. 625–27
> - Reflective Writing Assignments, pp. 627–32
> - Sample Reflective Essays, pp. 633–35

ASSIGNMENT GOALS

- To generate a learning narrative about your writing that candidly addresses successes, setbacks, realizations, and strategies for applying what you've learned to other situations.
- To illustrate your understanding of writing as a series of deliberate rhetorical choices that have effects.
- To apply what you've learned about analysis to your own writing.
- To gain critical distance from your writing in order to evaluate it and develop effective revision strategies.

ASSIGNMENT PURPOSE WITHIN THE 1001 CURRICULUM

This unit reinforces and formalizes reflection as a skill central to good writing. When we learn how to revisit our work after giving it some thought and gaining some distance from it, we are more likely to develop strong revising skills and become self-directed writers capable of re-entering an essay in order to improve and refine it. We believe that reflection nurtures habits that will serve you well in any writing situation.

MICROTHEMES

ENGLISH
COMPOSITION 1001

How We Read
Voice
Imitation
Style
Context
Genre

■ MICROTHEME ASSIGNMENT

Please note that the following assignments are short and focused (your teacher will give you specific instructions about length). They are designed to support the major papers you will be completing in each unit of your composition class. Instructors will select assignments that best complement their teaching style and approach.

Microtheme 1: How We Read

DISCUSSION

Although reading may seem like a skill you've already mastered by the time you come to college, the truth is that reading is a complex rhetorical process that we often take for granted. This assignment asks you to think very consciously about the process of reading and how it is influenced by the decisions that writers make to fulfill an intended purpose.

POSSIBLE ASSIGNMENTS

- Explain your reading process in relation to a text. Consider these questions: What was your first impression? As you continued to read, how did your impressions change, build, or get confirmed? What particularly about the text—the author's words and ideas, the format or structure, or other features—do you think was responsible for those impressions? Where did your interest wane and/or where did you find yourself being the most distracted and in need of refocusing your efforts? Given your responses, what sort of conclusions can you draw about the text, the writer, and you as a reader?

- Narrate your reading process with the goal of becoming conscious of reading as that which involves both mental and physical engagement. Narration might include any of the following: describe the scene where you're reading, including noise/distractions and other materials beside the text; describe rituals, if any, you have for the kind of reading you're doing; note when and why you pause/stop, if you do; and detail your reading strategies (i.e., when you pause to reread; when you read word-for-word; when you scan/skim, take notes, etc.). Based on this data, reflect on your relationship to reading. What assumptions do you bring to school reading? What are your strategies for successful reading?

- We can think about texts as performative, as doing things to readers that evoke emotional and physical responses. For this option, read aloud a piece of writing as if you were performing it for an audience and write about the choices you made in your performance, paying particular attention to how the text affected your delivery. You might choose to read a piece of writing with unusual punctuation or one that uses descriptive language—a poem or brief passage would work well. What gestures or facial expressions did you use and what body position or stance did you take? For example, how did you "perform" a dash or parenthesis? How did you portray the emotion or feeling behind a strong image or series of descriptive phrases? What does this performance help you realize about the reading process?

- Document and analyze a classmate's reading processes as he or she reads. Ask a classmate for permission to observe and ask questions about his or her typical reading process. Take careful notes as your partner reads, paying attention to how she is positioned, where her focus seems to wander, and where she seems most engaged or confused. Does the reader take notes or annotate the text? After she is done, ask questions about her reading process and the process of being observed. What about the observation and the reader's responses surprise you, and why? Explain what this activity suggests about useful and less useful ways to read a text.

- Describe an author's rhetorical moves, including attention to use of source material, connections between ideas, organizational logic, stylistic patterns, efforts to reach out to a particular audience, ways to prove his/her credibility, etc. Write about what you notice and reach some conclusions about the author's choices. Try to get a good grasp of how the text is put together and why. Think of it as a deliberately designed space: everything is there for a reason.

ASSIGNMENT GOALS

- To understand and appreciate the relationship between reader and writer.
- To view reading as a mental *and* physical activity that involves the whole person.
- To see writing as a process that requires practice, skill, and self-awareness.
- To recognize that texts make demands upon us as readers, and these demands shift based on style, genre, situation, and purpose.
- To understand the concept of rhetorical situation and be able to apply it to analysis of writing and reading practices.
- To develop meta-awareness of the choices that writers and readers in creating meaning.

Microtheme 2: Voice
DISCUSSION

Voice is a powerful tool in the act of persuasion. You need only think of your favorite singers to understand the pull of a strong voice, the way voices can bring people together, make them feel a common bond, and offer catharsis.

Writing has similar potential. Writing, authors Michael Berndt and Amy Muse say, "is not just self-expression; it is communication with the goal of affecting readers in real ways" (133). For the purposes of this exercise, your goal is for your reader to not just hear you but to be moved and affected by your words—so much so that they feel motivated to carry on your ideas in some way. You'll want to consider what strategies might help you to involve a reader in your experiences. What might help move them from their private concerns and attitudes to embracing your perspective, cause, or idea? You're working toward a conscious, strategic use of voice in this exercise.

POSSIBLE ASSIGNMENTS

- Choose a topic or issue and write a short text that aims to move your readers to care about it or to appreciate its importance. Include a one paragraph reflection on the choices you made: How did you consciously craft your voice and why? What specific characteristics of your voice did you pay most attention to (i.e., intonation, rhythm, emphatic word choice, and so forth)? What choices did you make in punctuation, imagery, and syntax, for example, to evoke a response. What do you see as the relationship between voice and purpose?

- Select a short text and recast it using a very different voice and attitude. Feel free to approach this playfully by using humor, exaggeration, persona, or digital programming like Xtranormal (http://www.xtranormal.com/). Reflect on how your recast allows you to reach a different audience and change the content of the message.

- Write a short analysis of an artist's use of voice that you find particularly compelling. You could select a writer, speaker, singer, or even a choreographer (whose voice takes a different form than the others). Explain what specific features of the voice make you return to the person's work.

- Record yourself using an audio recorder or your computer while reading aloud a passage from your own or another's text that you find particularly compelling. Feel free to record yourself reading several versions. In two paragraphs, write an analysis of your reading. Does your voice do justice to the passage? What, if anything, surprises you about the sound of your voice? What elements of the text are less or more compelling when you hear it aloud? Finally, reflect on how what you learned might translate to your writing.

RESOURCES

- Writer's Web: Clarity and Style http://writing2.richmond.edu/writing/wweb/voice.html
- zenhabits: Finding Your Voice http://zenhabits.net/voice/
- Peter Elbow: Voice in Writing Again: Embracing Contraries http://works.bepress.com/peter_elbow/23

ASSIGNMENT GOALS

- To understand that reading and writing are rhetorical activities with effects.
- To experience writing as a powerful medium for action.
- To appreciate and try out connections between voice and action.

Microtheme 3: Imitation

DISCUSSION

You've probably heard before that imitation is the sincerest form of flattery. It also happens to be a very useful strategy for learning new skills. For this exercise, you will work with a text, preferably one written in a style dramatically different from your own, by imitating its *strategies* (not its content; you supply your own content). Your goal is to experiment by trying to write in ways that may be new or even uncomfortable to you so that you might broaden your repertoire as a writer.

Through either revising a selection of your own work or creating an entirely new text, imitate a passage that you or your instructor chooses in one or more of the following ways. Be sure to indicate what you are imitating and why you chose the imitation you did: how does it relate to the purpose of your text, your intended audience, or other goals of your writing? What challenges do these differences approaches create for you?

POSSIBLE ASSIGNMENTS

- **Word use and sentence structure:** Capture some of the particular language the writer uses (disciplinary–specific words, spare descriptions, figurative language, etc.) and the variety or similarity of the grammatical structures of sentences. Look for key words or the use of certain parts of speech such as active or passive verbs, pronouns or proper nouns, the use or nonuse of adverbs and adjectives, and so forth.
- **Evidence provided:** Look at the range of evidence that a writer uses, including facts, statistics, hypotheticals, anecdotes, interview data, historical data or recollections, observations, quotations, cause–effect analyses, and images, including pictures. Notice also **how** the evidence is incorporated, such as in lists, through comparisons, or in visual forms such as graphs and charts.
- **Organizational structure:** Organizational choices can be obvious—such as the use of headings or a chronological delivery—or subtle, such as by juxtaposition or less obvious logical connections. Identify and imitate a particular organization within one paragraph or a set of paragraphs.
- **Rhythm:** Pay attention to the intonation pattern in a text (this might include using power words, cleft sentences, end focus, repetition, etc.). Imitate the rhythm, *not the content*. You might experiment with using nonsense words as Lewis Carroll does in "Jabberwocky," for example.

RESOURCES

Lewis Carroll "Jabberwocky" http://www.jabberwocky.com/carroll/jabber/jabberwocky.html

ASSIGNMENT GOALS

- To build a diverse repertoire of writing strategies by imitating others' writing.
- To appreciate the choices writers make for particular effects.
- To understand the relationship between stylistic and rhetorical choices and context, purpose, and audience.
- To experiment with language and have a little fun.

Microtheme 4: Style

DISCUSSION

These assignments focus on the interconnected nature of what we say and how we say it. In addition, the activities below foster a view of language as playful and fluid, not strictly rule-governed.

POSSIBLE ASSIGNMENTS

- Record a passage from any text; bold or underline every verb or verb phrase in the passage. Reread the passage after doing so and then write a character sketch of the writer based on the traits expressed to you through verb choices. Your task is to imagine the writer and construct a persona based on the feeling or sense that you get from the writer's verbs. Then, write an analysis of how you arrived at this description, making a special point to indicate the extent to which verbs influence the overall effect of the passage.

- Divide a piece of paper (or screen) into three columns. Mark the first column "what's being said," the second, "how it's being said," and the third, "commentary and invention." In the **first column**, record a passage (approximately a paragraph) of your own writing; beneath it, explain what you wanted to express in the passage, elaborating on and providing more context about the original. In the **second column**, analyze how you wrote the passage, commenting on your use of tone, style, voice, specific words, and sentence structures. In the **third column**, analyze the effectiveness of the "what" and "how." Do the two reinforce one another? Do they conflict? Does this passage sound on paper/screen the way you hear it in your head? Finally, also in this column, attempt a revision of at least one sentence from this passage and explain your goal for revising. Goals could include anything from a practical desire to better coordinate your thought and expression, to experimentation that allows you to try out a different approach.

- Keep a "commonplace" notebook of brief passages, quotes, sayings, etc., that convey interesting turns of language or ways of writing. Focusing on the *how* of the writing instead of the *what*, follow each example with your analysis of what makes the writing stylistically interesting to you.

ASSIGNMENT GOALS

- To experience the ways in which *how* something is written affects what we perceive about writers, characters, messages, and intent.
- To analyze what writers do to construct a persona and deliver a message.
- To develop an "ear" for reading and hearing different styles writers use.
- To experiment with changing language and style to produce different effects.

Microtheme 5: Context

DISCUSSION

All writing happens within a context. Rhetoricians reference the Greek word **Kairos** (καιρός), meaning the exact or critical time, opportunity, occasion, or season during which an action is most advantageous. In writing, then, a *kairotic* moment is a written response to an event or issue determined and bound by context, but context that is both of the moment and historically situated. This assignment asks you to consider how context influences a chosen text. For our purposes, we'll also include visual and spoken texts.

POSSIBLE ASSIGNMENTS

- Analyze a text's context and discuss how it affects other rhetorical elements. Context, broadly defined, is the set of circumstances surrounding an object of analysis. You will want to identify relevant factors such as:
  - date of writing, production, or publication
  - publication or dissemination type, genre
  - availability of the text
  - relevant pressing issues of the text's historical moment
  - ongoing debates related to the text's content
  - contemporaneous cultural concerns

Your goal is to come to an understanding of your text as part of a larger conversation.

Here are two assignments on context from Sharon Crowley and Debra Hawhee's *Ancient Rhetorics for Contemporary Scholars:*

- "Survey a variety of magazines and newspapers and select a handful of articles on a given issue. How does each article draw or create *kairos*? Is the issue so pertinent or urgent that little needs to be done to establish the article's relevance? Do some writers or speakers use an opportune moment to 'change the subject' and argue about a separate but related set of issues" (63)?

- "Choose an issue and read broadly about it, keeping track of the various perspectives. Then make a visual 'map' of the arguments, tracking how the main issue gives rise to others. The map may look like two sets of lists, or it may be more sprawling with lots of offshoots, like a broad web. Be sure to include in the map the arguments people are making, who the people are, and what values they seem to be asserting" (63).

ASSIGNMENT GOALS

- To see how responses to issues or events change over time depending on the circumstances or historical moment.
- To recognize that texts occur in reaction to various debates or conversations, and in turn, become part of the conversation.
- To notice the effects that context has on the style, rhetorical choices, or the genre of discourse.

Microtheme 6: Genre

DISCUSSION

Genres are the forms that discourse takes. Genres have particular conventions unique to their type. By understanding the conventions of a particular genre, writers are better able to meet the expectations of readers, and readers are better able to understand and respond appropriately.

POSSIBLE ASSIGNMENTS

- Examine several pieces of writing of the same genre—syllabi, lab reports, instructions, or blog postings, for example. Describe the texts you've selected as if they were objects by focusing on their appearance or components, instead of what they say. For example, notice the line breaks, lengths of paragraphs and sentences, spacing, use of italics, bold-face, bullet points, and so on. After describing how the texts look, write about what the appearance of the piece reveals about the expectations or conventions of the genre.

- Recast a genre in the form of another genre. For example, rewrite a horoscope or obituary in the form of a poem or a poem in the form of a recipe. Then write about what you did to recast the genre. How did the recast change your reading of the genre?

- Find two pieces of writing on the same subject written for two different purposes or audiences. Describe how the format, use of images, vocabulary, and so on, differ between the two texts.

ASSIGNMENT GOALS

- To understand that genres have conventions unique to themselves.
- To notice that genres influence how we write and read texts.
- To see how purpose and audience interact with the choice of genre.

EXAMPLE STUDENT RESEARCH PROJECTS

ENGLISH COMPOSITION 1001

Student Writing Samples

The following pages contain writing samples from several students who completed English Composition 102 (the second quarter version of English 1001) in 2011–2012. Their writing represents hours of thoughtful preparation and revision as they worked through their research project. You'll find samples of research steps, researched argument essays, recasts of their essays, rationales, and reflections. We wish to acknowledge and thank them once again for allowing us to publish their work.

Sarah Abellanida
Research Step: Determining a Research Topic
Research Step: Evaluating Internet Sources
Research Step: Annotated Bibliography
Research Step: Writing a Hypothesis
Research Step: Proposing your work
Researched Argument Essay: "Women, Media, and Politics"
Recast Project: Blog "Make me a sammich…women these days…"
Recast Project Rationale

> *Sarah Abellanida chose her topic because she wanted to write about something that mattered to her, in this case equality and empowerment for women. She saw the 2008 elections as an exciting moment that provided a stepping stone for women. She also wanted to talk about the election and how it was portrayed in the media. Sarah is an English major and is considering a marketing minor. Graduate school is a possibility with the aim of working in publishing, possibly as an editor.*

Julia Fallon
Research Step: Annotated Bibliography
Research Step: Outline
Research Argument Draft with Instructor Comments
Researched Argument Essay: "Honesty as a Policy"

> *Julia Fallon is a Communication Sciences and Disorders major. She is involved in a number of organizations, including UC's chapter of the National Student Speech, Language, and Hearing Association; Choose Ohio First Scholars; and the UC Chorus. She enjoys volunteering, performing music, and spending time with family and friends.*

Alexandra Land
Research Step: Outline
Research Argument Draft with Instructor Comments
Researched Argument Essay: "Arabs in the Media"

Alexandra Land is a Kolodzik Business Scholar majoring in marketing with a concentration in sales, and minoring in Spanish. She is an active member of Delta Sigma Pi and competes in sales competitions as a member of the UC Varsity Sales Team. She has co-oped at Precision Foods in St. Louis, MO in marketing strategy development. She enjoys traveling, spending time with family and friends, and discovering new music.

Laura Plikerd
Research Argument Draft with Instructor Comments
Researched Argument Essay: "Genetic Modification and the Issue of World Hunger"
Recast Project: "Famished" (Zine)

Laura Plikerd is a College Conservatory of Music student studying theater production. She has been involved with several organizations including the Racial Awareness Program (RAPP), Genderbloc, Serve Beyond Cincinnati, and UC's American Sign Language Club. Her interests include photography, traveling, cooking, and making costumes.

Taylor Smith
Research Step: Proposing your work
Research Step: Annotated Bibliography
Researched Argument Essay: "Standardized Tests: Every High School Student's Biggest Enemy"
Recast: Power Point slide show presentation
Recast Rationale
Reflecting on Your Work

Taylor Smith is currently an Exploratory Studies student, hoping to pursue a degree in Fashion Design. She is involved in Club Tennis. Her interests include traveling, sewing, tennis, and being with family and friends. She was passionate about her essay topic, why the ACT/SAT should be eliminated from college admissions, because she thinks using the tests as an admission standard disadvantages some students more than others. She also chose this topic because all students can relate to the experience of taking standardized tests.

Example Student Writing

Sarah Abellanida

English 102

Prof. Abby Fagan

Research Process Step: Determining a Research Topic

The impact of the Barbie doll on the female youth
-The Barbie doll is idolized by many young girls, and the Barbie doll incorrectly portrays a realistic view of how the average woman looks. I believe Barbie gives an artificial view of beauty.
-It's a topic that's been around for a while.
-How does Barbie affect young girls' views on beauty and perhaps the role of a woman in general.
-That Barbie is a harmless toy, and social environments are too different to generalize Barbie has an effect on the majority of the girl population.

How women are portrayed on TV
-That actresses chosen are usually the stereotypical "beauty", and that TV should try being more realistic (minus the reality TV).
-Watching TV.
-Why does society seem to idolize the actresses on TV? Why does television feel the need to use their beauty as a tool for ratings?
-That everyone reacts to beauty no matter what, and that television has the right to boost their ratings anyway they want to.

How women in a position of power are seen
-That women perhaps still don't have the same respect as men do. I believe that women aren't seen as much of a power symbol as men are, although they should be.
-Articles in magazines and segments on the news.
-Why aren't women given much credit when in a position of power?
-That women are equal to men, and that women suffrage has already secured that reasoning.

Sarah Abellanida

English 102

Prof. Abby Fagan

Research Process Step: Evaluating Internet Sources

Abramson, Elise. "Barbie Brains: The Effect of Barbie Dolls on Girls' Perception of Male and Female Jobs." 21 May 2009. Web. 8 Jan. 2012.

Date, Publication. "PLoS ONE: Being Barbie: The Size of One's Own Body Determines the Perceived Size of the World." PLoS ONE : Accelerating the Publication of Peer-reviewed Science. Web. 08 Jan. 2012.

"Early Adolescents' Experiences With, and Views Of, Barbie | Adolescence | Find Articles." Find Articles | News Articles, Magazine Back Issues & Reference Articles on All Topics. Web. 08 Jan. 2012.

Halliwell, Emma, Helga Dittmar, and Suzanne Ive. "Does Barbie Make Girls Want to Be Thin? The Effect of Experimental Exposure to Images of Dolls on the Body Image of 5- to 8-Year-Old Girls." 2006. Web. 8 Jan. 2012.

"Study: British Girls Mutilating Barbies : NPR." NPR : National Public Radio : News & Analysis, World, US, Music & Arts : NPR. Web. 08 Jan. 2012.

"Voice of Reason: Research Debunks 'Barbie Ideal' | LiveScience." Science News – Science Articles and Current Events | LiveScience. Web. 08 Jan. 2012.

I believe these websites would all be helpful to my research project because they all have information vital to my research paper. Each website seems to be unbiased and therefore credible. I think that these websites would suffice for a good chunk of knowledge for my research paper. Thus I deem all these websites usable for my paper.

Sarah Abellanida

English 102

Prof. Abby Fagan

Research Process Step: Annotated Bibliography

Works Cited

Baird, Julie. "The 'Palinazation' of Palin." Newsweek [New York] 30 Nov. 2009: 26. Print.

This article is about sexism in media, and focuses mainly on Sarah Palin. The article talks about the term "Palinazation" and how many women in the media now are using the term for when they feel the media is demeaning them. The article also brings into light, although Palin had been commented on her looks and lifestyle, being coined, "Caribou Barbie" she also made many flukes and was not yet ready or experienced to be in a position of power to be running our country.

This article relates to my topic, because not only does it talk about sexism in the media, but it also brings into light that perhaps, although Palin was "Palinized" in the media, perhaps in some aspects she had it coming. She doesn't have the merit really to be running a country, and in fact seems to "Palinize" other women as well. Ideas I had while reading this is perhaps candidates or women in politics are not just being victimized because of their gender, but perhaps because they truly can't run a government. This article seems to be credible the author quotes sources such as CBS news.

Cocco, Marie. "RealClearPolitics - Like Hillary, Sarah Faces Media Sexism." *RealClearPolitics*. 15 Jan. 2012. < >.

This article focuses mainly on Palin and the negative attention she received in the media. It mainly highlights a lot of what the media had said about her, quoting the terms such as, "caribou barbie" and talks about how she became a sort of idolized "sexual object". This article mainly just talks about how the media went extremely far in how they portrayed Palin during the length of the Presidential election.

This article relates to my topic because it's focusing on the media and how it's portraying a vital woman in the government, or was in the government. This article pulls quotes from sources like CBS news and Katie Couric, and also brings into question how far is the media willing to go?

"Did Sexism Do Michele Bachmann In?" *The Daily Beast*. Web. 15 Jan. 2012.

This article mainly focuses on Michelle Bachman and her most current run for presidency candidate for the republicans before dropping out. The article details her many, many deficiencies. Not shying away from saying that she more or less was a bit wacky, and was more than obviously not a good choice for presidency. But then when it looks towards her losing Iowa, and coming in dead last, the article shows that a main cause of it was due to sexism and the fact that voters, in Iowa, just couldn't fathom a woman president.

This article relates to my topic because it shows that although Michelle Bachmann was overly eccentric and spouted out a many of untruths during her republican candidacy run, that perhaps she was under fire of sexism as well, for there is always a market of voters for even the crazy things she seemed to say. This article quotes voters in Iowa who claim that it was in fact not her crazy, but her gender, as the reason why they did not vote for her in the republican presidential candidacy. This gives me an idea of the whole personality and credentials versus gender debate.

Kim, Jane. "Let's Talk About Sex(ism)." Columbia Journalism Review Nov.-Dec. 2008: 12-14. Print.

This article talks about sexism in the media, and focuses towards the 2008 elections. The author focuses more towards Palin than Hillary Clinton and describes the differences in criticisms between the two politicians from the media. As Hillary Clinton was seen as a "bitch" and was seen with a tough exterior, Palin was seen as the "soccer mom" and described as "beddable".

This article definitely relates to my topic because I'm able to pull from it not only quotes from the media, but also quotes from Geraldine Ferraro, who was the first woman to appear on a major party ticket, and that allows me to compare what she says about sexism and media to replies from Palin and Clinton. This gives me the idea that perhaps I should look into women who have been in the government in the past, and perhaps look at the history of sexism and politics.

"Michelle Obama Tired Of 'Angry Black Woman' Stereotype." Breaking News and Opinion on The Huffington Post. Web. 17 Jan. 2012.

This article focuses on Michelle Obama and the current "angry black woman" image she is being portrayed with in a new book that currently came out about the Obama family. It shows that even a woman in power like the madam president is under fire in the media. And the fact that she was portrayed as an angry black woman is an ultimate sexist and definitely racist term.

This article relates to my topic because it goes beyond just women in politics, or just women running for president, but extends to women of power. Although Mrs. Obama is not a politician, she is still under fire from the media, showing that sexism is still a part of normalcy in the media and everyday life. This article pulls quotes from the book, and from Mrs. President herself. Also this gives me the idea to look at other first ladies in the past and see if any of them were under scrutiny, for example Hillary Clinton.

Seelye, Katharine Q., and Julie Bosman. "Media Charged With Sexism in Clinton Coverage - NYTimes.com." *The New York Times - Breaking News, World News & Multimedia*. 15 Jan. 2012. Web. 15 Jan. 2012.

This New York Times article is about the media coverage during the 2008 presidential campaigns and how the media seemed to attack then Senator Clinton and used many sexist remarks and comments about her. This article mainly focuses on the media, and how the media seemed to talk about topics which no other candidate would ever be punished for such as, "showing cleavage". In general the main points are that the media seems to come out looking unfair when covering Hillary Clinton compared to covering other candidates, even Barack Obama.

This article relates to my topic by showing that perhaps the candidates aren't only being shown up by their appearances or mainly for being women, but also because they perhaps are not worthy of candidacy. The authors Katharine Q. Seelye and Julie Bosman use many good, reliable sources. They use many direct quotes from very well-known and then very present news casters during the 2008 campaign such as, Katie Couric. They also quote many different sources such as a Democratic party chairman, a newscaster on NPR, a panelist on MSNBC, a political correspondent for CBS news, and many more. I believe this source is very credible. I can't seem to find a shred of bias in this article. Not only do they show the sexist remarks and facts that show them, but they also include studies that show that Senator Clinton was close in the running to Senator Obama, now President Obama towards the end of her presidential run. Ideas I get from this article is to focus on what the media has to say on the topic. Do they see themselves as being unfair, or do they believe they are just reporting the news and doing the public a favor?

Tannen, Ben. "Media Perpetuates Sexism in Presidential Race | Yale Daily News." *Yale Daily News - The Nation's Oldest College Daily*. Web. 15 Jan. 2012.

This online article from the Yale Daily News is mainly about sexist remarks aimed towards current Secretary of State, and former senator and presidential candidate, Hillary Clinton during the 2008 elections. In general his main points were that Hillary Clinton was given too much negative attention during the election period for simply being a woman, and that a big factor to the negative sexist attention was mainly caused by the media, not necessarily the voters or viewers. In conclusion he feels that this was simply wrong and hopes for this to be eradicated.

This article relates to my topic. It talks about Hillary Clinton mainly. The author does seem to quote some reliable sources, such as the New York Times, and he brings into light different facebook groups that were created to dissuade voting for the current Secretary of State. Although he seems to have a few reliable sources, and gives first person accounts of his own experience, he does admit to supporting Hillary Clinton, so there shows some bias on his part. This gives me the idea to see what the voters think. Do they give in to what the media says, and play into their little games, or do the voters have a better sense than that?

"Women in Government: Clare Boothe Luce." GovLoop - Social Network for Government. Web. 01 Feb. 2012.

"AfterEllen.com - Condoleezza and the Comic Strip Controversy." News, Videos & Reviews on Lesbian & Bisexual Women | After Ellen | Lesbian Celebrities in Entertainment, TV & Movies. Web. 01 Feb. 2012.

Homan, Paul. "Geraldine Ferraro Dies at 75 | NBC New York." New York News, Local News, Weather, Traffic, Entertainment, Breaking News. Web. 07 Feb. 2012.

Sarah Abellanida

English 102

Prof. Abby Fagan

Research Process Step: Writing a Hypothesis

Roles:

#1- The media reports the news and is not sexist.

-Are the female politicians really being singled out more than the male politicians? If so, is it intentional?

　　-Female candidates are getting as much air time as male political. Every candidate has something that they can claim to be a victim of, whether it be gender, race, religion or etc. So if a woman politician is being singled out perhaps it's on the demerits of her political stance.

-Does the media see any difference in their air time for female politicians and male politicians? Is it all negative?

　　-The media does not give female politicians more air time, in fact the reason that there are more male politicians then they are given more air time. The fact that there are less female politicians in the government then it may look like their air time is negative because when they are called out it looks like their only air time is negative media since they have so little of it compared to the male politicians who are the majority.

#2- The media singles out female politicians, and they are victims of sexism.

-Why does the media choose to single out the female politicians?

　　-America is still in the mindset that women are not as functional as men. This is shown in the mere fact that plenty of other governments have had women presidents where as there is a minority of women in our government.

-Are the voters and viewing audience becoming influenced by the news feed? If so, how does this affect their political views?

　　-The viewing audience at home of course is becoming influenced because the news is their main source of information, whether it be televised or literature. This of course affects their political views because viewers are too lazy or too busy to do their own research on the politicians themselves.

Sarah Abellanida

English 102

Prof. Abby Fagan

Research Proposal

This research paper is a main focus on women politicians and how they are portrayed through the media. My claim is that the media concentrates way too much on the image of these women, and don't give them the credit they deserve. Although the mainstream media can at times victimize all women, I choose to put more of an emphasis towards the women politicians in our government. I choose to do this because these are women who hold actual power within our country. They have authority to change our lives and the fact that women make up 51 percent of the population, yet only make up 17 percent of our congress is staggering. What's even more astounding is that only 3 percent make up the House of Representatives when compared to the equivalent of Rwanda where they have 56.3 percent according to MissRepresentation.org. The fact that the United States government is 235 years old and not once has a women resided in the 4 year term as President is odd, especially since there is 193 countries currently making up the United Nations, 2 independent states and a few other self-declared nations and only 27 of those nations is currently being ran by a female leader, according to guide2womenleaders.com.

I plan on first concentrating on the 2008 presidential elections. This was the first real turn in the United States political history when it came to female politicians. This was the first time that a woman, Hillary Clinton, made a serious move to becoming the first female president of our nation. Not only was Hillary the first serious woman politician to run for candidacy, but Sarah Palin as well was the first woman to run as Vice President. As I look into the 2008 election I'll focus my topic towards the media and how they portrayed both Clinton and Palin. It is more than obvious that both were victims of media sexism. What is more interesting is how both women received negative attention, but in two completely different ways. Clinton portrayed more as a ball buster whereas Palin was portrayed as "Caribou Barbie". Now many subtopics can spring from looking into the 2008 election. I plan on comparing how Clinton was portrayed before she ran for candidacy. She was not only a senator, but also a president's wife, she had the credentials for presidency. The question here is, was Clinton always viewed as a "ballbuster" with "cankles" and a "cackle" like a witch, or did this only come into view when she stepped into the limelight as a candidacy runner. As for Palin, I plan on looking into how she was viewed during the run for presidency and after the election. In Palin's case, the question isn't whether she was viewed differently, although I'm sure she was, but whether she was victimized because of her credentials or because she was a woman on rise for power.

That of course would lead into the question, does the media choose to attack these women of power because of their position of influence and the feeling of them being in power is threatening, or because they truly do not have the credentials. Neither reason is acceptable to allowing sexism in any manner, but perhaps finding the reason as to why the media chooses to victimize these women, or "Palinize" as the term seems to be now a days, then we can find ways to purge ourselves of it completely. The main politicians I would focus on in this area of my paper would be Sarah Palin and Michelle Bachman. Although biased, I find that these two women seemed to have the least amount of credentials, and seemed to have spouted the more extravagant claims during their time in the media's limelight. I would compare them to other women politicians and compare how they were portrayed. Palin was viewed as a "MILF" and Michelle Bachman was a witch. These both seem like the more extreme portrayals, closely followed by Condaleesa Rice being labeled a "dominatrix" after wearing a black outfit, including a leather skirt, and Michelle Obama currently being stereotyped as an "angry black woman".

I then plan on looking at the history of women in politics. Had these women have to face the same crimes put against them as the females today? If so, what was done to put an end to it? Was anything said or done at all? I have a quote from Geraldine Ferraro, who was the first woman on a major party ticket, and she seems to claim that there was indeed sexism very present back then. That then springs the question, was it as strong as it is today? Were the voters or viewing audience appalled at all, or was it just all a part of the norm?

Next I plan on looking at the media's stance on the issue. Do they see their reporting as sexist or do they just see it as them doing their job and reporting the news? I would then look at the fact that women only hold 3 percent of clout positions in the mainstream media according to MissRepresentation.org. Does this mean that since the media is technically run by mostly men, that this is a main reason for why women aren't given enough professional credit, and given more bodily insults? I also would like to look into whether there are reporters out there who also see this as a problem, not only women, but men too. I will look into Katie Couric, the first woman to become the main anchor of a nightly news station, and then perhaps try to compare what she has to say to that of men anchors and reporters. Do men and women both see this as a problem? What are the differences?

I would then probably fall into my concluding paragraph. Possibly bring into light that perhaps sexism is used as a tool to get politicians noticed, or to put them in a negative light? Had Palin overly complained about her being a victim, customizing the word "Palinization"? As a victim had she used her negative attention to get more attention? If so, had this turned into even more negative attention? What are other women in politics doing differently to not receive such negative attention? Possibly I would talk about what should be done about sexism in the media, but then that would lead into too many issues such as censorship. Then perhaps I'll spit out a couple of random facts such as how only 3 percent of the fortune 500 CEO's is made up of women, or how women only compromise 7 percent of directors and 13 percent of filmmakers in the top 250 grossing films to show that it's not only in politics that women seem to be lacking in presence and perhaps if there were more women in politics, then the world, or more specifically, the United States would be more comfortable having women in power in all areas of profession.

The paper is due February 8, and the first few pages are due the 30th. So then I guess I have already started my research, but I'll begin my writing my paper the 26th.

Sarah Abellanida

English 102

Prof. Abby Fagan

8 February 2012

Sexism Plaguing our Media and Politics

In 2008 *Saturday Night Live* premiered the first episode of their 34th season. The opening sketch of the premier episode was an awe inspiring historical moment for SNL. It was the second most watched episode since September 2001 and amassed around 10 million viewers that night. The set opened up to a much missed Tina Fey acting as Sarah Palin and an almost eight month pregnant Amy Poehler acting as Hillary Clinton. The two women not only made SNL history because it was one of the most watched episodes, but ironically they were embodying the true history being made in the United States at the time. Never had there been a woman on both major party tickets at the same time, running for such prestigious positions as they were. Poehler and Fey joked their way through an invented PSA announcement about sexism within the presidential campaign, and although the skit was fantastically written and excruciatingly funny, it came to a serious note with Amy Poehler's closing line, "…it is never sexist to question a female politician's creden-tials…" (Fey 215). This brings into light the question: had the media executed their job of doing just that? Thinking back to the 2008 presidential elections what does one think when reminiscing about Sarah Palin? To many, the terms "Caribou Barbie", "Hockey Mom" and perhaps even "MILF" spring to mind. I don't know about others, but nothing about these terms scream credentials to me. So this brings us back to the question: does the media fulfill their job of reporting the news or are they, just like *Saturday Night Live*, merely in it for the ratings? Although it may be hard for some to admit, sexism is very real within our media, and a little too real within our government.

The media has been utilizing sexism as a tool for decades, and what makes this worse is that America has not quite caught on to it yet. Back in 1942 Claire Booth Luce ran

84

for Representative of Connecticut on the Republican ballot using the platform that Franklin D. Roosevelt had brought the United States into WW2 unprepared, and openly compared FDR's concession to that of Joseph Stalin's hold on Eastern Europe (Homan). She won her campaign with great ease even though she was an open foe of FDR and his New Deal policy. During her time in the House of Representatives, she had her legs voted second most beautiful in a newspaper poll. She was asked about the "dignity of congress" and responded by stating, "Don't you realize, Congressman, that you are just falling for some subtle New Deal propaganda designed to distract attention from the end of me that is really functioning?"(Baird). Of course the publicity of Luce's legs overshadowed all of her anti-FDR campaigning, which worked in FDR's favor, who eventually went on to win the presidency. America may look at what happened to Claire Booth Luce and blame the era. The 1940s were a time where women had a certain role in society, and that role tended to keep them in the kitchen, not in congress. But, what about our contemporary era? How is voting Claire Booth Luce's legs second most beautiful any different from CNBC's Donny Deutsch claiming Sarah Palin to be "totally beddable", or the *Washington Post* commenting on Hillary Clinton's cleavage or even *The Oklahoman* commenting on her "frequent wearing of dark pants suits to conceal her bottom-heavy figure" (Heimer). If not for the only difference that Claire Booth Luce's victimization had a little more class to it, the media really has not progressed at all.

It is more than obvious that during the 2008 presidential campaign both Hillary Clinton and Sarah Palin were victims of sexism through the media. What is more interesting though is how both women received negative attention in two completely different ways. Clare Booth Luce had said, "Women who are considered feminine will be judged incompetent, and women who are competent, unfeminine . . . who succeed in politics and public life will be scrutinized under a different lens from that applied to successful men" ("Clare Booth Luce Biography"). The 2008 presidential election was a turning point in American history when it came to female politicians. This was the first time that a woman, in this case Hillary Clinton, made a serious move to becoming the first female president of our nation, as well as Sarah Palin who was the first woman to run for the Vice Presidency on the Republican ballot. Clinton and Palin's experiences within the campaign seem to embody Claire Luce Booths' quote, stated above. Palin, who was portrayed as the beautiful and "beddable" one, had become the focus of many jokes, and was not taken seriously for she could see "Russia from her window." Clinton was portrayed as the ballbuster and a she-devil with no emotion. Tucker Carlson, a panelist on MSNBC, had stated that, "when she [Hillary Clinton] comes on television, I involuntarily cross my legs" (Seelye and Bosman). It is interesting to see how although both women encountered it differently, they both were maltreated for their different personalities and were stereotyped into two different categories. Although interesting, it was still wrong, and these stereotypes played a part in the loss of their elections. When voters watch or read the media and see these women demeaned, they then choose to not take them seriously, because who would want a ditz as a vice president or a bitch for commander and chief.

The corruption of the media not only affects the viewers and the voters, but could it have plagued our politics and politicians as well? As Hillary Clinton received negative attention as a bitch, a ballbuster and even a dominatrix, Sarah Palin seemed to work off of the image the media portrayed of her, using it to her advantage, or at least tried to. Just as FDR used Claire Booth Luce's legs as propaganda, Sarah Palin was merely doing the same thing, but to herself. This of course brings up the question: what does being a hockey mom have to do with politics? The answer: it doesn't. Palin spent two terms being a mayor of Wasilla, Alaska and barely two terms being a Senator before campaigning with McCain. Compared to Hillary's eight years as first lady, almost two terms as a senator and a graduate of Yale Law School, Palin didn't quite equal up to Clinton's credentials, yet she still climbed her way through the polls alongside McCain. With all the publicity that Clinton and Palin received, the public can sometimes forget about other female politicians, and may overlook the victimization that they too had gone through way before these two. Geraldine Ferraro was the first woman to appear on a major party ticket. She, like Palin, ran for vice presidency in 1984 alongside Walter Mondale. She told Newsweek in an interview that when she became a victim of sexism she "couldn't speak about it" (Baird). In contrast was Palin, parading around in it, coining the new phrase "Palinization". Palin had cornered the sexism market as her own. Some could argue that Palin was witty and turned a negative into a positive for women, using her femininity to her advantage to work with the media. Others though found Palin's actions to be degrading. As Kim Jane stated in her article "Let's Talk About Sex(ism)", "had Ferraro trumpeted her mothering skills, she would have been hooted off the stage", perhaps that's because mothering skills have no place in politics, even though America still seems to prefer women in this role. It seems odd though that even with this mothering deposition Palin still fell short of becoming what America thought of as an appropriate choice for vice presidency. If the mothering type was not what America wanted, then it is strange that Clinton fell short with her portrayal as emotionless and strict. It seems that no matter what manner a women decides to depict herself as in the Political arena she will be scrutinized.

Our nation has settled into a mindset that women come last, that we should allow men to lead and women should follow in their shadow, but this theory is barbaric. Condoleezza Rice, the former secretary of state, was the focus of a "Boondocks" comic strip, which implied that if she "had a man in the world who [she] truly loved, then she wouldn't be so hell bent on destroying it" (Warn). Not only does this comic strip degrade Rice, but the whole female population by implying that women are frigid and destructive unless they have a male counterpart. It is this mindset that fuels sexism in the first place. Nancy Pelosi the first and former female speaker of the house claims that for women in the government sexism just "goes with the territory" (Homan). It does not and definitely should not be this way.

It seems for every step the female population takes towards equality, we get knocked back five more. If one woman fails then she is not the only one who bombs, but the entire population bombs with her. Clare Booth Luce once stated, "Because I am a woman, I must make unusual efforts to succeed. If I fail, no one will say, 'She doesn't have what it takes'; They will say, 'Women don't have what it takes'" (Homan). Well, it is now the 21st century, but it feels as though our nation is still stuck in that 1940s mentality. Palin and Clinton are far from being the only ones victimized or "palinized" within the media. Even the current first lady Michelle Obama, four years after the infamous 2008 election, is under attack. She is stereotyped as an "angry black woman" in *New York Times* reporter, Jodi Kantor's, new tell-all book about the Obama administration. She received this stereotype because she allegedly butts head with some of the top advisers within the White House. Not only is this term sexist, but it is also racist. What does it say for our nation in this modern era that Jodi Kantor, a professional woman herself, could use such a sexist term?

The sad truth is that sexism has beleaguered many female politicians, and if women don't have each other's backs, then how could we ever expect men to? Just recently Michele Bachman dropped out of the Republican candidate race. Citing sexism as the reason for Bachman's recent downhill spiral may be a stretch, since she was the politician who hinted towards the "Lion King" as being gay propaganda and that carbon dioxide was "harmless" (source?). However, in "Did Sexism Do Michele Bachmann In," *The Daily Beast* points out that Bachman, who seemed likely to win big in Iowa, had a "dismal showing", thus leading her to drop out of the race. "I've noticed that when her name is mentioned sometimes that there's a lot of men that wouldn't vote for a woman," commented an Iowa county GOP chair ("Did Sexism"). An Iowan woman who was a former supporter of Bachman stated, "I just started thinking about being presidential and I don't know that we're ready for a woman for president" ("Did Sexism"). What does it say about our nation when a woman herself can say that we are not "ready for a woman president"? How can women reach full equality if our own gender is the one holding us back? This statement demonstrates a nation full of stereotypes and close-mindedness, and only shows how we, along with the media, have not advanced either when it comes to sexist remarks.

It would be nice to erase sexism completely from our society, but at this point in time it is close to impossible. Perhaps we could start by eradicating sexism from our media and our newsfeed. According to MissRepresentation.org women only hold 3 percent of clout positions in the mainstream media, so perhaps the fact that the media, like the government, is mostly run by men is the reason that sexism is so strong within media corporations. When Hillary Clinton spoke up about the sexism that was orbiting around her campaign, Rem Reider, an editor of the American Journal said, "she [Hillary Clinton] had a long track record in public life as a serious person and a tough politician, and she was covered that way" (Seelye and Bosman). However, does this give the media reason to point fingers and call names? Katie Couric, a woman who herself has been under this same kind of scrutiny for being the first lone woman newscaster of an evening news program, commented on Clinton's reaction stating that "one of the great lessons of that campaign is the continued — and accepted — role of sexism in American life, particularly in the media" (Seelye and Bosman). Even Candy Crawley, a reporter for CNN, confessed that when it came to sexism she "certainly did see it in the commentary" (Bosman and Seelye). We cannot dance around the issue that sexism is real, and is probably here to stay for a number of decades to come, but perhaps through regulating the media we could slowly change the sexist mentality that is currently influencing not only viewers and voters but our nation as a whole.

Through modern day technology it has become much easier for Americans to communicate and receive their information. As Andew Kohut of the Pew Research Center states, "Americans are spending more time with the news than over much of the past decade. Digital platforms are playing a larger role in news consumption". The media seeps through this technology and lodges itself into the publics' brain. How can one help reading a sexist term and not keep from falling into that sexist attitude? It is almost impossible to keep one from doing so. Would regulating the media really be so bad? The idea being proposed is not to censor the media, but to standardize it, and to define the fine line between reporting the news and commenting on petty gossip. I believe that with adjustment of the media's conveyance of news in order to eradicate sexist remarks from it completely will in turn slowly wean the American public from the sexist mentality. Perhaps a result will be a woman president.

Sadly though, with the media running rampant, women must take a backseat for now. Even though we make up 51 percent of the population it is staggering to know that only 17 percent of our congress is female ("Miss Representation"). What should be even more astounding is that women make up only 3 percent of the House of Representatives, compared to the equivalent of Rwanda, where 56.3 percent are women ("Miss Representation"). The fact that the United States government is 235 years old and has not once had a women reside in the 4 year term as President is odd compared to the 27 nations out of the 193 countries currently making up the United Nations, 2 independent states and a few other self-declared nations which are currently being ran by a female leader ("Worldwide Guide"). Although 27 out of 193 is a small ratio, do you not think that America should be a part of that small percentage at one point? Perhaps without all the "palinization" that the media has flaunted around for the last few decades America would have joined the flanks of other countries who have had women leaders long ago. Geraldine Ferraro once commented in an interview to *Ladies Home Journal*, after losing to Reagan, "I don't think I'd run again for vice president," and after taking a pause to laugh continued to say, "Next time I'd run for president" (Kim). With sexism still plaguing our country and our newsfeed, there really is no hope that America will be jumping on that bandwagon. That is unless the media is given better regulations, and sexism is completely wiped from our news feed. Then and only then could women have the ultimate equality in this country and lend a hand at leading it.

Bibliography

Baird, Julie. "The 'Palinazation' of Palin." Newsweek [New York] 30 Nov. 2009: 26. Print.

Cocco, Marie. " Like Hillary, Sarah Faces Media Sexism." *RealClearPolitics*. Web. 15 Jan. 2012.

"Did Sexism Do Michele Bachmann In?" *The Daily Beast*. Web. 15 Jan. 2012.

"Worldwide Guide to Women in Leadership." Worldwide Guide to Women in Leadership. Web. 1 Feb. 2012.

Heimer, Katie. "Hillary Clinton and the Media: From Intelligent and Fair to Appallingly Sexist and Pointless." National Organization for Women (NOW). Web. 21 Feb. 2012.

Homan, Paul. "Geraldine Ferraro Dies at 75." NBC New York. Web. 07 Feb. 2012.

Kim, Jane. "Let's Talk About Sex(ism)." *Columbia Journalism Review* Nov.-Dec. 2008: 12-14. Print.

Kohut, Andrew. Pew Research Center for the People and the Press. Web. 07 Feb. 2012.

"Michelle Obama Tired Of 'Angry Black Woman' Stereotype." *The Huffington Post*. Web. 17 Jan. 2012.

"Miss Representation." Miss Representation. Web. 1 Feb. 2012.

Seelye, Katharine Q., and Julie Bosman. "Media Charged With Sexism in Clinton Coverage." *The New York*. 15 Jan. 2012. Web. 15 Jan. 2012.

Tannen, Ben. "Media Perpetuates Sexism in Presidential Race." *Yale Daily News*. Web. 15 Jan. 2012.

Warn, Sarah. " Condoleezza and the Comic Strip Controversy." *After Ellen*. Web. 01 Feb. 2012.

Abellanida 9

"Women in Government: Clare Boothe Luce." GovLoop. Web. 01 Feb. 2012.

Women in History. "Clare Booth Luce Biography." Lakewood Public Library (Lakewood, Ohio). Web. 1 Feb. 2012.

Sarah Abellanida

English 102

Prof. Abby Fagan

Recast and Rationale

Recast: http://makemeasammichwomenthesedays.blogspot.com/

My intended audience is male. I am trying to aim more towards the eighteen to about thirty year mark. My audience is still considered relatively young, and still in bachelorhood. My type is more of less the stereotypical "frat boy" character. The type of man with the "women cannot drive" mentality and probably lives in an apartment full of guys or maybe even moved back to live with his parents in their garage or basement. My audience is of course still hip to the current media and mildly keeps up with current events, most likely from watching the Colbert Report.

The form of my recast is a blog and the original idea was to do a website, but the feedback I received from many was that a blog would first of all be easier to set up, but also it would allow me to inform but also include my own opinions. I agree with the feedback, I feel it is easier for readers to connect to the text when it seems as though someone is speaking to them. By doing the recast in the form of a blog instead of a website I am able to still give my audience facts, but in a way that doesn't seem forced or even boring.

I feel a bit restricted with my blog only because I know I am writing for a certain audience, and usually when writing a blog it is more of a diary type situation, so you can usually just write then people who are like you will read it, but in this situation it is the reverse. I have to write a blog for a specific targeted audience and hope that they read it. So my writing style is a bit different than usual, just because I do not want to come off too feminine or come off sounding too die hard and put off my audience. I feel like the easy going, almost nonchalant style is what will read well with my audience best.

My hook for the recast is sort of using the sexist remarks but like twisting it around. I am still playing around with a title for the blog, but currently the one I have is "Make Me a Sammich…Women These Days". The title I feel is serious and sort of plays off of that age old joke about women only being good for making sandwiches. The background of my blog is also a picture of a sandwich, which I also feel is a good way to hook in an audience, because the sandwich looks really delicious. Either they will stay to read the blog or go eat something. Then when it comes to my blogs I start off using titles that will engage them, like one is titled "Cougars, Milfs and Babes…oh my", and I got this idea from the feedback I received. The guys I talked to said that if they read certain words then it makes them want to stay and read, the example I was given was "doggy style", but I am finding it a bit difficult to work that into my blogs. Then my actual blogs are just me breaking up pieces of my paper and going even more into depth with the paragraphs, and I try to keep it light hearted and try not to come off as some die hard liberal feminist, which I hope I am doing okay at, because I really am not a diehard liberal feminist at heart.

Difficulties I am running into is trying to find a way to create this blog without coming off seeming sexist towards men. I really am only going off what male feedback has told me, and in a way it is supposed to be a bit humorous using sexism as a joke to help get the point across. I think perhaps I may have over thought it in a way that it may go over some people's heads. Another main difficulty I have come across is that I find that when I write, I write a lot. My posts are a bit winded, and I hope I do not end up losing my audience for that fact. Also, the time management is strenuous, because it feels as though I need to bust out tiny essays on my topic every few days, which is fun, but with all the other homework I have on my plate is a bit nerve wracking.

Example Student Writing

Julia Fallon

Professor Ris

English 102 TH 9:30

8 May 2011

Wikileaks: An Annotated Bibliography

Goldsborough, Reid. "The New Age of Investigative Journalism?" *Teacher Librarian* 38.2 (2010)

- Addresses numerous, varied perspectives
- People might lose their jobs or lives due to information on WikiLeaks
- Acknowledges the idea that WikiLeaks is a "data dump"
- Suggests that WikiLeaks is operating at "the highest level of journalism"

This article from the peer-reviewed journal "Teacher Librarian" describes Wikileaks as it relates to the media and investigative journalism. Due to the fact that the information revealed via Wikileaks is done so through the internet and brought to attention by the popular media, it is worth discussing the popular media's role in the Wikileaks debate. It offers a unique perspective in regard to Assange's role as an investigative journalist, suggesting that he is simply doing his job. Reid's purpose is to inform readers of the various opinions on Wikileaks and the website's implications on the media.

Calabressi, Massimo. "Wikileaks War on Secrecy: Truth's Consequences" *Time*. 2 December 2010.

- Raises the question of whether governments should analyze their actions in response to WikiLeaks
- The repercussions of the WikiDump have the ability to change history
- Addresses the idea that "People rely on confidential communications to do their jobs"
- Raises the question of whether or not governments can rely on confidentiality in the age of WikiLeaks
- President Obama is having difficulty rebuilding the credibility of our government

This article from "Time" provides a comprehensive resource of information about Wikileaks which will be highly useful in summarizing Wikileaks and the controversy surrounding it. It aims to provide a very general description of Wikileaks and touches on the various stakeholders and issues within the debate. This article is particularly useful in my research essay because it deals directly with Wikileaks as it relates to the idea of secrecy within governments.

Schmitt, Eric. "In Disclosing Secret Documents, Wikileaks seeks 'Transparency.'" *The New York Times* 25 July 2010. Print.

- Includes Assange's quote that "transparency in government activities leads to reduced corruption"
- Discusses negative cricitisms from the military and the government
- Addresses the idea that Assange manipulates information (suggests the idea of self-promotion)

Eric Shmitt's article in "The New York Times" is helpful with the Wikileaks controversy in the way that it uses numerous quotes from the stakeholders involved, including one from Julian Assange himself. These quotes provide a more specific perspective, rather than just a general description of the debate. This article aims to provide more exact details about the Wikileaks controversy and offers more information about those who are impacted by the information being released. This is useful for my research essay because it allows me to draw even more information about the implications of releasing confidential information and the potential effects it can have.

Greenwald, Glenn. "The War on Wikileaks and Why it Matters." Salon.com. *Salon*. 27 March 2010.

- Explains the government's extremely negative attitude toward WikiLeaks and why the Pentagon aims to take WikLeaks offline
- Stands behind Assange's view that the release of information promotes national security
- Uses Iceland as an example of a government that has collapsed due to corruption
- Defends WikiLeaks on the grounds that it is highly effective investigative journalism

This article from salon.com provides a unique perspective to my research essay in the way that it is highly opinionated and persuasive. Greenwald is clearly a proponent of Wikileaks and believes that Assange is providing information that citizens have a right to know. It is important to include the opinions of specific individuals since the Wikileaks debate has so much to do with citizen's rights. While some of my sources suggest that Assange has been unethical in his actions, this source offers the opposite opinion.

Assange, Julian. Interview by Andy Greenburg. The Firewall. *Forbes*. 29 November 2010.

- Touches on the idea of Julian Assange being a self promoter
- Explains the repercussions of WikiLeaks on large corporations
- Reveals Assange's belief that government's keep secrets in order to scare people and maintain control

This interview of Julian Assange by Forbes' Andy Greenburg is extremely useful to the Wikileaks debate because it provides opinions on releasing confidential information from the master himself: Julian Assange. This interview is also unique because it discusses Wikileaks in terms of its effects on businesses (rather than simply describing the governmental leaks). However, it still offers useful information in terms of Assange's intents with Wikileaks and his stance on confidentiality. Greenburg's purpose appears to be trying to uncover Assange's reasoning behind exposing information from corporations and businesses and also to reveal the effects that Wikileaks has had on large corportions.

Julia Fallon

Professor Ris

English 102 TH 9:30

8 May 2011

Wikileaks: A Research Essay Outline

I. Attention-getting Opener: Imagine a society where nothing is kept secret from its citizens, no matter what the repercussions may be. Thanks to Julian Assange and his controversial website "Wikileaks," that society is more than just an idea, it is a possibility and a reality.

1. **Thesis:** Controversial as it may be, one thing is certain: the irreversible release of confidential information via Wikileaks has set the stage for an important debate regarding the ethics of confidential information within the government and its relationship to national security.

II. Topic Sentence: Since 2006, WikiLeaks has been releasing classified government information; while always heavily criticized, the real controversy began when the organization released thousands of documents regarding military operations (Source: New York Times).

- WikiLeaks hosted the largest release of classified information in history (Source: Time).
- The military says it jeapordizes operations and government officials accuse Assange as simply being a self promoter (Source: New York Times).

III. Why exactly do governments deem so much information confidential?

- Confidential information can be useful in the way that it can have a profound impact on the way certain situations play out.
- Confidential information can also be used to shape public opinion; if all information is available to citizens, then managing public perception would be made significantly more difficult.
- However oppressive that may sound, an effective government should have the support of it's people; therefore, perception management is important.

IV. Topic Sentence #2: Assange insists that the release of confidential information is vital to national security.

- Assange himself said that "transparency in government activities leads to reduced corruption" (Source: New York Times)
- Assange has spent a lot of time in Iceland, where they support his belief that "investigative exposure" promotes national security; this belief is pervasive due to their recent economic collapse based on corruption (Source: Salon).
- Assange believes that governments scare people in order to control them; WikiLeaks is trying to undo that ideology. (Source: Forbes)

V. Topic Sentence #3: While Assange insists that his actions are ethical, many argue the opposite: that the release of confidential information is exactly what threatens national security.

- The more leaks he receives, the more his own profile rises (Source: Forbes).
- According to Hilary Clinton "people rely on confidential information to do their jobs" (Source: Time)
- Instead of promoting national security, WikiLeaks causes distrust toward governments and hostile attitudes (Source: Time).
- Assange has failed to mention important details within his leaks that often make things worse than they appear (Source: New York Times)

VI. Topic Sentence #4: Investigative journalism is all about revealing the truth to citizens. Does this mean that Assange is simply doing his job?

- Some say that WikiLeaks is operating at "the highest level of investigative journalism" (Source: Teacher Librarian)
- The decrease in print press has correlated with a decrease in investigative journalism; therefore, Assange is simply doing the hard work that most writers on the internet are no longer willing to do (Source: Teacher Librarian.)
- On the other hand, there is a fine line between doing one's job and doing the right thing when people's jobs and lives are at stake.
- Ultimately, however, it is possible that WikiLeaks is over-sensationalized, due to the fact that it is simply an information dump (Source: Teacher Librarian).

VII. Topic Sentence #5: Assange's intents aside, the information now exists and governments are forced to address it.

- The government is now forced to analyze what should be kept secret and how many secrets it should have in the first place (Source: Time).
- It is important to analyze how citizens opinions of their governments rely on both their access to information and the content of that information.
- The presence of WikiLeaks has the potential to shape government actions.
- Government's should ask themselves whether they are doing more harm than good by keeping confidential information from its people.

VIII. Conclusion: While WikiLeaks may be slightly unethical in its practices, it does not change the fact that governmental confidentiality needs to be addressed. Perhaps it is not about revealing all information, but it seems that governments could benefit from keeping less classified information.

Julia Fallon

Professor Ris

English 102 TH 9:30

9 May 2011

Title?

Unclear

Imagine a society where nothing is kept secret from its secrets, no matter what the repercussions may be. Thanks to Julian Assange and his controversial website "WikiLeaks," that kind of society is more than just an idea; it is a possibility and a reality. Since 2006, WikiLeaks has been causing distress to international governments by leaking confidential information to the public. With simply access to the Internet, citizens now have the ability to unlock secrets regarding their government's foreign relations, environmental actions, and even military operations. However, the debate on WikiLeaks has to do with more than simply politics; it has direct implications on our rights as citizens to know our government's actions. While many believe that citizens have a right to access this information, others believe that secrecy exists in governments in order to protect its people. Controversial as it may be, one thing is certain: the irreversible release of confidential information has set the stage for an important debate regarding the ethics of confidential information within the government and its relationship to national security.

Simple? Only?

You need the set the stage. What was the Wikileaks that was already known? What are they and who was doing this?

While WikiLeaks was known for releasing classified information, its recent release of thousands upon thousands of documents regarding US military operations (among other various issues) has been the most controversial. Its release of these "diplomatic cables" was the largest illicit publication of confidential information to date (Calabresi). Suddenly, the entire world had the ability to browse videos, documents, and communications

How can you identify the time-frame further and what this is in relation to what had been leaked already?

regarding international foreign relations, most notably the Afghan war. The US government military has a viable reason to worry; the details of war are not often pleasant, and a country relies the support of its people in times of war. Officials in these areas are concerned that the WikiDump infringes on the privacy rights of some individuals and compromises military operations (Schmitt). However, WikiLeak's leader, Julian Assange, disregards this fact. The organization is founded upon the belief that candid exposure of information to people will create more honest, ethical governments. His intent, he stated, was to expose the "unethical behavior" of governments, which he saw as necessary for citizens to be aware of (Schmitt).

> More on what is being leaked needs to be noted here or by the various stakeholders.

> You're using Schmitt a lot and we don't know who this is in order to judge whether Schmitt's interpretation of the officials and Assange's perspectives are accurate. Also these each need more development as they are crucial to understanding the controversy.

In light of the WikiDump, a major issue being debated is the reason as to why the government has so many secrets in the first place. Firstly, the withholding of certain information can have a profound effect on the way certain political situations play out. In Time Magazine's article "WikiLeaks War on Secrecy: Truth's Consequences," Massimo Calabresi uses the example that if "Confederate General Robert E. Lee's [had] not been found wrapped around cigars by Union troops," the results of the battle might have been significantly different. However, Calabresi also makes the argument that while it is necessary to keep some information classified, today's governments classify all too much information. He suggests that an overabundance of secrets within a government ultimately "diminishes the credibility of the government's judgement about what should be secret" (Calabresi). In "The War on WikiLeaks and Why it Matters," Glenn Greenwald accuses the government of relying on secrets to maintain control through an idea called "perception management." While Greenwald speaks unfavorably toward perception management, suggesting that government's do not have the right to manipulate information in order to appear more ethical to

> Who is this?

> Unclear what's being talked about here.

> Who are we talking about? In both these cases, it would take someone who is an expert to identify whether or not the government is, in fact, withholding unnecessary information or at least that certain sectors believe this to be so and therefore add to the controversy.

Incomplete sentence

No apostrophe

its people. However, others say that it is crucial for government's to have the support of their people in order to be effective. In his article published in The Nation, Jordan Stancil states that secrecy is necessary for governments to have the ability to provide helpful intervention to other nations. This suggests that classified information is crucial for effective international affairs to take place.

Can you categorize one set of controversies as whether or not what is withheld in the first place should be withheld? Then noting who the players are here would be useful.

Julian Assange insists that the release of confidential information lessens corruption and is vital to national security. Eric Schmitt, in his article in The New York Times refers to a quote from Assange himself: "We believe that transparency in government's leads to reduced corruption, better government and stronger democracies." Assange alludes to the fact that WikiLeaks seeks to provide justice and keep governments in check. According to scholar Evgeny Morozov in his interview with New Perspectives Quarterly, WikiLeaks is based on the theory of "[minimizing] the power of government's to do things their citizens do not know of and may not approve of." By exposing information to the general public, WikiLeaks aims to halt corruption in its early stages, rather than allowing it to progress and worsen within its walls of secrecy. Glenn Greenwald of Salon supports WikiLeak's position using the example of Assange's choice to spent a significant amount of time in Iceland. Iceland, Greenwald states, is the recent victim of a "full-scale economic collapse" as a result of corruption. "Numerous nefarious causes . . . were hidden completely from the public and even policy makers" Greenwald says, until corruption worsened to the point where complete financial ruin became inevitable. Iceland's support of WikiLeaks in light of its recent instability represents a notable situation in which something like WikiLeaks could have been beneficial.

According to whom?

While Assange insists that his actions are beneficial, his opponents argue the opposite: that the release of confidential information is exactly what threatens national security. If everyone, including foreign leaders, is aware of a country's intentions, then measures taken by a government to protect its people could be futile. Leaks on foreign relations can also interfere with a nation's ability to intervene in international affairs as well as human rights cases (Stancil). If every single action taken by a government is released to the public, foreign relations could easily become strained if there are disagreements. Unsurprisingly, political figures have held hostile attitudes against WikiLeaks; jobs and lives are potentially at stake as a result of the WikiDump due to the content of some of the leaks (Goldsborough). This fact emphasizes the necessity of considering the safety of those individuals directly involved with the leaks, rather than just our own personal rights as citizens to know that information. Mary Kay Cary of U.S. News and World Report addresses another chilling detail: that the WikiDump included "sensitive sites" that could be "potential targets for terrorists. It is understandable (and even comforting) that a government would want to classify such information, as its release jeopardizes our national security.

[Next paragraph will discuss the repercussions of the leaks and the implications of the new "Internet Freedom." I will address investigative journalism and discuss the concept of "whistle-blowers" in the media]

You should identify your sources so we can judge these ideas more carefully.

Disagreements by whom?

Where is the end of the quote?

This was supposed to be a complete draft.

Works Cited?

Julia,
For what you have so far, we need to have a better understanding of what Wikileaks are before we understand or can judge the various perspectives about it. I'm not quite sure I understand what you are considering to the controversy itself that is being considered. See also my marginal comments.

Prof Ris

Julia Fallon

Professor Ris

English 102 TH 9:30

9 May 2011

Honesty as a Policy

Imagine a society where nothing is kept secret from its citizens, no matter what the repercussions may be. Thanks to Julian Assange and his controversial website "WikiLeaks," that kind of society is more than just an idea; it is a possibility and a reality. Since 2006, WikiLeaks has been causing distress to international governments by leaking confidential information to the public. With access to the Internet, citizens now have the ability to unlock secrets regarding their government's foreign relations, environmental actions, and even military operations. However, the debate on WikiLeaks has to do with more than just politics; it has direct implications on our rights as citizens to know our government's actions. While many believe that citizens have a right to access this information, others believe that secrecy exists in governments in order to protect its people. Before WikiLeaks, citizens were aware that classified information existed, but they are now able to see what kind and how much information, thus setting the stage for a unique but important debate. Controversial as it may be, one thing is certain: the implications of WikiLeaks have raised an important question regarding whether confidential information is a necessity for national security or a barrier that is preventing honest governments.

WikiLeaks has been responsible for the largest illicit publication of confidential information, referred to as "diplomatic cables," to date, according to *Time* government reporter Massimo Calabresi in his article about the varied consequences of the release of this kind of information. While WikiLeaks was targeted since its beginnings for releasing classified information, its recent release of thousands upon thousands of documents regarding US military operations (among other issues) has been the most controversial. Suddenly, the entire world had the ability to browse videos, documents, and communications regarding international relations, most notably the Afghan war and the War in Iraq (Calabresi). The US government and military has a viable reason to worry; the details of war are not often pleasant, and a country relies the support of its people in order to intervene in international affairs. However, WikiLeaks' founder, Julian Assange, disregards this fact and makes his intentions clear. As a form of investigative journalism and revolutionary activism, the ultimate goal of WikiLeaks according to Assange is to make all, not just some, government information known to the public. The organization is founded upon the belief that candid exposure of information to people will create more honest, ethical governments. Eric Schmitt, in his article in *The New York Times* refers to a quote from Assange himself: "We believe that transparency in governments leads to reduced corruption, better government and stronger democracies."

According to WikiLeaks, if all information were released to the public, governments would be held more accountable for their actions. This would, in the opinion of the organization, promote national security. Assange alludes to the fact that WikiLeaks seeks to provide justice and keep governments in check. According to Stanford University scholar Evgeny Morozov in an interview for *New Perspectives Quarterly*, WikiLeaks is based on the theory of "[minimizing] the power of governments to do things their citizens do not know of and may not approve of" (Morozov 8). By exposing information to the general public, according to Morozov, WikiLeaks aims to halt corruption in its early stages, rather than allowing it to progress and worsen within its walls of secrecy (10). That is, if governments knew that their every action would be exposed, they would act in more ethical ways; therefore, the corruption that fuels conflict would be stopped before it had a chance to start. Glenn Greenwald, a lawyer, columnist, and blogger, supports WikiLeak's position using the example of Assange's choice to spend a significant amount of time in Iceland. Iceland, Greenwald states, in an article for *Salon* entitled "The War on Wikileaks and Why it Matters," is the recent victim of a "full-scale economic collapse" as a result of corruption. Greenwald notes that, "Numerous nefarious causes . . . were hidden completely from the public and even policy makers" until corruption worsened to the point where complete financial ruin became inevitable. Iceland's support of WikiLeaks in light of its recent instability represents a notable situation in which something like WikiLeaks could have been beneficial.

A major source of controversy surrounding WikiLeaks was the sheer amount of information that was released. WikiLeaks operates under the principle that no information should be confidential; therefore, it exercises unsystematic dumping of information with hopes to achieve secret-free governments. The number of documents released by WikiLeaks numbered in the thousands, this reflects the massive amount of information that is kept classified by governments. As a result, some individuals are less upset with the content of the information and more concerned about the amount of information that was being kept a secret. Massimo Calabresi, in his article in *Time.com*, argues that today's governments classify all too much information. He suggests that an overabundance of secrets within a government ultimately "diminishes the credibility of the government's judgment about what should be secret" (Calabresi). According to this view, secrecy could potentially create mistrust toward governments. This problem is made even more problematic by the issue of control with which Glenn Greenwald is concerned. Greenwald accuses the government of relying on secrets to maintain control through an idea called "perception management." The more information a government keeps confidential, the more control it has over its people; therefore, if the actions of a government are unethical, it can remain in control as long as it keeps those actions a secret among government officials.

While Assange insists that his actions are beneficial, his opponents argue the opposite: that the release of confidential information is exactly what threatens national security. If the entire world is aware of a country's intentions, then measures taken by a government to protect its people could be futile. Classified information can have a profound effect on the outcome of certain situations, especially military operations. Massimo Calabresi explains how this could have resulted in major changes in the outcomes of events that we, perhaps, take for granted and don't realize are often the result of what information is kept secret or is exposed. For example, if "Confederate General Robert E. Lee's orders [had] not been found wrapped around cigars by Union troops," the results of the battle might have been significantly different (Calabresi). While many argue that war should not exist at all, it is a harsh reality; ultimately, many feel that it is better to be protected by the military rather than to have its operations to do so infiltrated and dismantled. In his article in *The Nation*, Jordan Stancil, a lecturer in the Graduate School of Public and International Affairs of the University of Ottawa, writing on the connections between WikiLeaks and security of our government, suggests that leaks on foreign relations can also interfere with a nation's ability to provide helpful intervention regarding other nations or human rights cases. If every single action taken by a government is released to the public, foreign relations could easily become strained if there are disagreements among powers.

Unsurprisingly, political figures have held hostile attitudes against WikiLeaks; jobs and lives are potentially at stake as a result of the leaks due to the content of some of the information that was revealed (Goldsborough). This fact emphasizes the necessity of considering the safety of those individuals directly involved with the leaks, rather than just our own personal rights as citizens to know that information. Mary Kate Cary, in the opinion section of *U.S. News and World Report* addresses another chilling detail: that the information leak included "sensitive sites" that could be "potential targets for terrorists" (Cary). These included many high-profile installations such as "hydroelectric dams, vaccine production facilities, and communication hubs" (Cary). Many of these sites would put individuals involved in the government in serious danger, as well as our nation as a whole. It is understandable (and even comforting) that a government would want to classify such information, as its release directly and unarguably jeopardizes our national security. Officials in the military and international affairs also argue that WikiLeaks directly infringes the privacy rights of some individuals (Schmitt). In a country where individual rights are highly valued, eliminating rights to privacy would be counterproductive to our nation's emphasis on civil liberties.

No matter how heavily criticized or fervently praised, it is impossible to undo the release of this information, the implications of which must now be addressed by governments. In an age where the Internet has made information so readily available, should governments modify their actions in response? Scholar Evgeny Morozov suggests that Assange could potentially be the leader of a movement based on "the principles of absolute 'Internet freedom,' [such as] transparency [and] very permissive copyright law" (Morozov 9). After all, WikiLeaks has serious implications on the Internet, given that it was the sole source through which the leaks were released. Therefore, Morozov suggests that WikiLeaks might have less to do with diplomacy and more to do with intelligence gathering and sharing (Morozov 9). It is not necessarily surprising that an organization like WikiLeaks would emerge from the Internet, which sets a new standard for freedom of speech. In an era where "Internet freedom" is practically a reality, it is arguable that secrecy will become decreasingly possible; thus, it seems that governments need to embrace openness in order to survive.

Many believe that the emergence of WikiLeaks could usher in a new age of transparency in governments, just as Assange had intended. The key would be to find the middle ground that exists between "the culture of secrecy that dominates now and the kind of indiscriminate dumping that seems to be the goal of Julian Assange," according to Jordan Stancil. Certainly, WikiLeaks has made it so that governments must now analyze all of the information they have deemed secret in the past; perhaps, many hope, the controversy surrounding the website will lead officials to determine whether or not that information should have been classified in the first place. However, the pervasive opinion that governments should become less secretive and more ethical does not seem to be playing out; the Obama administration has been forced to "tighten, not loosen, its security protocols" in order to save face (Calabresi). Only time will tell the amount of classified information will be reduced in response to WikiLeaks. For now, damage control is the primary focus of government officials.

In times of global political turmoil, the concept of whistle blowing in the media is nothing new. However, WikiLeaks should not be written off as just another form of investigative journalism, nor should Julian Assange be dismissed as a crackpot. Never before has an organization been so successful in releasing so much information, and its implications extend far beyond the scope of what other investigative journalists have done. WikiLeaks' goal is complete transparency, and whether the organization will achieve this goal, no one knows. However, the questions raised have certainly forced governments to at least reconsider their previous actions and citizens to reconsider their rights. Does confidential information protect its citizens or create hostility? Should citizens have the right to access that information regardless? The answers to these questions are worth debating. They have the ability to create a unique conversation among citizens worldwide that could ultimately lead to a more shared set of values regarding secrecy, and whether ethical or not, we have WikiLeaks to thank.

Works Cited

Calabresi, Massimo. "Wikileaks War on Secrecy: Truth's Consequences." *Time.com* 2 December 2010. Web. 11 March 2011. <http://www.time.com/time/magazine/article/0,9171,2034488,00.html>

Cary, Mary Kate. "The Real WikiLeaks Threat." *U.S. News and World Report*. Opinion. 9 Dec 2010. Web. 4 March 2011. <http://www.usnews.com/opinion/articles/2010/12/09/the-real-wikileaks-threat-is-julian-assange-just-a-guy-with-a-laptop-or-a-cyber-terrorist>

Goldsborough, Reid. "The New Age of Investigative Journalism?" *Teacher Librarian* 38.2 (2010): 57. *Professional Development Collection*. Web. 21 Apr. 2012.

Greenwald, Glenn. "The War on Wikileaks and Why it Matters." *Salon.com*. Salon. 27 March 2010. Web. 2 March 2011. <http://www.salon.com/2010/03/27/wikileaks/>

Morozov, Evgeny. Interview. "WikiLeaks and the Perils of Extreme Glasnost. *New Perspectives Quarterly* 28.1 (2011): 7-11. Print.

Schmitt, Eric. "In Disclosing Secret Documents, Wikileaks Seeks 'Transparency.'" *The New York Times online*. 25 July 2010. Web. 2 May 2011. <http://www.nytimes.com/2010/07/26/world/26wiki.html>

Stancil, Jordan. "On WikiLeaks and Government Secrecy." *The Nation*. 3 December 2010. Web. 12 May 2011. <http://www.thenation.com/article/156835/wikileaks-and-government-secrecy>

Example Student Writing

Alexandra Land

Professor Ris

English 102

10 May 2011

Outline

Introduction

I) Attention-Getter

   1) Opening lyrics to *Aladdin*

      A) "Oh, I come from a land, from a faraway place, where the caravan camels roam, where they cut off your ear if they don't like your face. It's Barbaric, but hey, it's home."

   2) Disney's animated film, *Aladdin*, was the company's first movie with Arabic roots.

   3) With magic carpets, a genie, and spans of deserts, Disney had used the common stereotypes to portray the Arabic culture as alien and harsh compared to the Western cultures.

II) Thesis

   1) The media in the United States is perpetuating Arab stereotypes causing a prejudice against Arab-Americans.

Body

I) Arabs have been falsely depicted in American media since the 20th century.

   a. The common Arab image was inherited to America by British and French traders who traveled to the Middle East in the 1800's (Jhally).

      i. As Americans, "We took them, embellished them" (Jhally), into exotic stereotypes.

   b. Today, common themes are presented in Arab images.

      i. The Arab-American Anti-Discrimination Committee (ADC) compiled a list of popular stereotypes used in the media. On that list includes common slander such as camel jockeys and towel-heads, notions of foreign activity like belly dancing or terrorism, and descriptions of negative personification like greedy, dirty, uneducated, and violent.

      ii. In fact, "more than 300 movies, nearly 25 percent of all Hollywood movies" (Reel Bad Arabs), degrade the Arab culture by using images such as these.

      c. With the American film industry contributing "more than $180 billion an-
nually to the U.S. economy" (MPAA), it has a heavy influence on how the
American society will determine what is socially acceptable.

II) The influence of American media allows for negative stereotyping of Arab
Americans to become commonplace in societal thinking.

      a. The media's impact on the ideas of society can be explained with the acces-
sibility principle.

            i. The accessibility principle states that people make social judgments
"based on the information that come to the mind most readily [and]
the more frequently a construct [image] is activated, the more accessible it becomes" (Persson & Musher-Eizenman).

            ii. Put to practical use, when the media constantly portrays the Arab
culture negatively, the average person will be more likely to produce
the same negative connotation rather than a more factual depiction.

            iii. These distorted views in the media, paired with recent historical
events (Palestine/Israeli Conflict, Arab oil embargo, and the Iranian
Revolution), create a fear towards the Arabic culture.

III) Islamophobia has emerged as a new social fear in non-Arab American cultures.

      a. Although social scientists do not have a clear definition of this new fear, the
common concept consists of a fear towards those who practice Islam and
individuals commonly associated with the Middle East.

      b. In an article by blogger, Daniel Tutt, he shares the research from Gordon
Allport on the psychological aspects of stereotypes.

            i. Allport found that stereotypes are used to respond to inner anxieties
towards "out-groups" (Tutt), in this case Arab-Americans.

      c. Jack Shaheen, an activist against vilifying the Arabic culture in the media,
commented that, "Words such as Arab and Muslim are perceived as threatening words…The stereotype has become…invisible to people [because]
we've grown up with these images" (Jhally).

      d. *Hate crimes? Discrimination?

IV) Using negative stereotypes of the Arab culture in film influences the Arab-American culture as well.

      a. The media directly affects the self-esteem of Arab Americans.

            i. The ADC found that Arab-American children tend to feel inferior or
ashamed of their culture due to lack of education devoted towards
their culture in school, stereotypes formed as humor, and cases of
bullying.

V)   Hollywood continues to vilify Arabs in film, because society has accepted the negative stereotypes.

    a. With Islamophobia rising rapidly after 9/11, depicting Arabs as villains are psychologically accepted,

        i. "There's not going to be any pressure on any producer who makes a film vilifying Arabs... There's a double standard....Hollywood is sort of clinging to this stereotype" (Shaheen).

Land 1

Alexandra C. Land

Professor Ris

English 102

19 May 2011

Arabs in the Media

"Oh, I come from a land, from a faraway place, where the caravan camels

roam, where they cut off your ear if they don't like your face. It's Barbaric,

but hey, it's home."

The opening lyrics to Disney's *Aladdin* transported the audience

from the dark, cool, musty theater to the dry, open, magical land of the

Middle East. *Aladdin* was the first animated Disney film that focused on

the Arab culture. Just like film makers before them, Disney added magic

carpets, belly dancers, and oppressive men to capture the essence of

the Western-coined term of "Arab Land". With the film industry in the

United States claiming a wide influence on society, these so called "Arab

Land" portrayals are an important source for American ideas of the Arabic

culture. Unfortunately though, the Western portrayal of the Arabic culture

is erroneous; no, there have not been any magic carpets discovered. This

erroneous portrayal has cemented harmful stereotypes into the American

society causing a fear towards Arab-Americans. Arab-Americans, the

general society, and Hollywood are affected by the usage of negative Arabic

stereotypes.

Arabs have been falsely depicted in American media since the

20th century creating stereotypes defining a culture. The common Arab

image was inherited to America by British and French traders who traveled

to the Middle East in the 1800's (Jhally). As Americans, "We took them,

More seriously than this, erroneous portrayals have . . . (I'm not sure if magic carpets have done this, so you want to move away from that comment.)

Generally good opening

It may be better to start with identifying the way in which Arabs have been depicted, without characterizing them as good or bad. Otherwise, I find myself thinking, what's bad about showing belly dancing, which

114

embellished them" (Jhally), into exotic stereotypes. Writers and storytellers added fantasies filled with dangerous adventures and beautiful women to the traders' tales. Today, common themes have developed as staples presented in Arab images. The Arab-American Anti-Discrimination Committee (ADC) compiled a list of popular stereotypes used in the media. On that list includes common slander such as camel jockeys and towel-heads, notions of foreign activity like belly dancing or terrorism, and descriptions of negative personification like greedy, dirty, uneducated, and violent. Other common stereotypes include the "oil sheik" with a thick accent donning a turban, a faceless woman suppressed by a veil, and incompetent terrorists plotting to undermine the United States and its allies. And what about the Arabic heroes? They have Anglo-Saxon features, lighter skin than the "bad guys", and an American accent (Wingfield). The American film industry has standardized a false depiction of the Middle East that is influencing the American society.

Americans are exposed to high levels of media influence. With the American film industry contributing "more than $180 billion annually to the U.S. economy" (MPAA), it has a heavy influence on how the American society will determine what is socially acceptable. Also, Americans spend more time watching television and going to movies than ever before. After the U.S. Census Bureau released the 2007 Statistical Abstract of the United States, experts found staggering reports in the amount of media exposure adolescents and elementary children are receiving. The document reported by that "average youth 8 to 18 years old spends almost seven hours every day plugged in to the media" (Beg). The report includes types of media such as the Internet, film, television, video games, and popular literature such as

---

Margin notes:

is something not indigenous to the US, or representing women in veils, which is what some Arab women wear. The next paragraphs can pick this up and explain why some see this as negative and while others defend it. It's hard to come to the defense of something you've already characterized as false and stereotypical and slanderous.

What do we mean by the media? Since you started with Disney, it's hard not to read this as movies; if not, tell us a range of places these depictions are found in.

Be sure you clarify other media outlets that also depict Arabs in certain ways; as noted above, the examples sound like the movies—you begin and end on that note (Disney to your last sentence in the previous paragraph). Unless this is clear, readers could say the fictional world of the movies is clearly balanced by other representations.

magazines. With such a wide variety of media bombarding adolescents with different images and messages, it is easy to absorb and accept the media's content quickly rather than spend time processing the value of the content. So, at a time period where adolescents are beginning to explore their environment outside of the household, they are being exposed to violent images of different cultures, the Arab culture being one of them, that tamper with logical judgment.

Can you place this sentence in a more active mode? This makes it unclear how this normal thinking arises.

The influence of American media allows for negative stereotyping of Arab Americans to become normal in societal thinking. The media's impact on the ideas of society can be explained with the accessibility principle. The accessibility principle states that people make social judgments "based on the information that come to the mind most readily [and] the more frequently a construct [image] is activated, the more accessible it becomes" (Persson& Musher-Eizenman).

Connect somehow to avoid a fragment starting with "meaning"

Meaning, when the media constantly portrays the Arab culture negatively, the average person will be more likely to produce the same negative connotation first rather than a more factual depiction.

Some groups arguments? One reason for the controversy? This may actually be a good transition/ topic sentence for the next paragraph. Transitions belong in the paragraph they describe.

These distorted views in the media, paired with recent historical events (Palestine/Israeli Conflict, Arab oil embargo, the Iranian Revolution, and 9/11), create a fear towards the Arabic culture.

Popular stereotypes that the media portrays of the Arab culture have lead to an acceptance of fear. In an article by blogger Daniel Tutt, he shares the research from Gordon Allport on the psychological aspects of stereotypes. Gordon Allport is an American-born psychologist who founded the idea of trait theory of personality. Allport found that stereotypes are used to respond to inner anxieties towards "out-groups" (Tutt), in this case Arab-Americans. An out-group is the group that is outside a person's societal norm of interaction. People will naturally revert to stereotypes to cope with confrontation of an out-group. If the stereotypes that come readily to mind are negative, such as in the case of the Arab culture, a person is more likely to consider a that group sub-human and express feelings of hate, dislike, fear, or other undesirable feelings. Jack Shaheen, an activist against vilifying the Arabic culture in the media, commented that, "Words such as Arab and Muslim are perceived as threatening words…The stereotype has become… invisible to people [because] we've grown up with these images" (Jhally). By combining the theory of the accessibility principle with Allport's ideas on stereotypes, it is clear on how islamaphobia has emerged as a new social fear in non-Arab American cultures. Although social scientists do not have a clear definition of this new fear, the common concept consists of a fear towards those who practice Islam and individuals commonly associated with the Middle East. The American society, in general, instantly reacts negatively towards images of the Arab culture which causes issues of discrimination. Because the "bad Arab" image is so commonplace in America, most people do not notice how frequently, and inappropriately, it is used, but in reality, "more than 300 movies, nearly 25 percent of all Hollywood movies" (Jhally), degrade the Arab culture by regurgitating the Western-born stereotypes.

Are these solely contemporary movies or do they represent older movies that had a habit of depicting many "foreign" individuals inaccurately (including Japanese, Africans, etc.)

The American media is indirectly encouraging negative attitudes towards Arab-Americans, becoming the source of violent hate crimes. After the attack on the World Trade Center in 2001, hate crimes and other physical discrimination tactics have been used on Arab Americans. The ADC reported that over 700 hate crimes were documented in the weeks that followed 9/11 (American-Arab Anti-Discrimination Research

Institute 12). Although reports of hate crimes have decreased since the initial year after the terrorist attack, levels of violent discrimination are still significantly higher than pre-9/11 levels (American-Arab Anti-Discrimination Research Institute 12). The ADC also continues in the report to note that most cases of violence towards the Arab Americans did not start as an intention of harm, but rather as an altercation. These altercations then escalated for racial stereotypes and slurs against Arab-Americans were used (American-Arab Anti-Discrimination Research Institute 12,13). Because the

Examples?

media can be linked as a vital contributor to islamaphobia, the non-Arab Americans involved in the attacks were recalling their instinctual knowledge of the Arab culture first: fear. The media's portrayals of "Arab Land" are coming to the person's mind more readily than a rational depiction. Also, instead of reducing the stereotypical roles of Arabs in movies to subdue

Examples?

cultural tensions, Hollywood actually produced "scores of films… that are clearly 'post-9/11 movies' in the sense that they encode and attempt to manage anxieties and concerns that are directly connected to the emotions and affects the attacks generated in American minds" (American-Arab

This needs support, especially in the contention that the media is encouraging violence against Arabs and Arab-Americans.

Anti-Discrimination Research Institute 77). Hollywood has combined the established stereotypes of "Arab Land" of pre-9/11 with the anxiety and fear birthed from the terrorist attack on 9/11 to produce even more films that falsely depict the Arab culture. By doing this, the film industry is indirectly approving a fear based on inaccurate stereotypes.

Using negative stereotypes of the Arab culture in film influences the Arab-American psychology as well. The media indirectly affects the self-esteem of Arab Americans. The ADC found that Arab-American children tend to feel inferior or ashamed of their culture due to lack of education devoted towards their culture in school, stereotypes formed as humor among, and cases of bullying. Carrie Conaway studied the psychological effects of stereotypes. She found that a person's performance is dependent on the stereotypical norm of the activity. If Arab-American children are constantly exposed to images degrading their culture or only images of Anglo-Saxon heroes, it can be theorized that the Arab-American children will feel inadequate to succeed leading to a lack of achievement. This lack of achievement will not affect the Arab-American community, but it will as affect society as a whole for it is expected to be higher unemployment rates, increased crime, and little contribution to the educational fields.

> Good argument against negative stereotypes

Why would the media industry continue to use negative Arabic stereotypes if it is clearly cause psychical and mental distress for Arab Americans and a recipe for an unbalanced society? For a profit.

Hollywood continues to vilify Arabs in film, because society has accepted the negative stereotypes. Hollywood has had a long track of degrading the popular out-group of the era. African Americans, Jews, and Catholics have all been negatively portrayed in film. In today's society, with Islamaphobia rising rapidly after 9/11, depicting Arabs as the "new" villainis psychologically accepted, "There's not going to be any pressure on any producer who makes a film vilifying Arabs… There's a double standard…. Hollywood is sort of clinging to this stereotype" (Shaheen). The intent of any business is to make a profit. In the film industry, making a profit means playing on the emotions of the audience to believe a story. In modern America, especial the twenty-first century, the general society is willing to except an Arab as a villain. For film makers, it is too enticing to use the pre-packaged villain of the Arab instead of fighting the protest from the audience if, for example, a Jewish American was used.

The media in the United States has influenced the general society to believe in negative Arabic stereotypes. Even though Hollywood could potential suffer monetarily by withholding these negative stereotypes, society, as a whole, would profit. The general society will no longer be subject to degrading images that could influence harmful behavior. Meanwhile, the Arab-Americans would see a decrease in the overall discrimination rate. The American society would see *a whole new world (Aladdin)*.

Works Cited

American-Arab Anti-Discrimination Research Institute . Report on Hate Crimes and Discrimination Against American Arabs: 2003 and2007." (2008). 12,13,77. Web. 17 May 2011. <http://www.adc.org/PDF/hcr07. pdf>.

Beg, Sami. "Mass Media Exposure." ABC News: *Health* 15 Dec 2006. Web. 18 May 2011. <http://abcnews.go.com/Health/story?id=2727587&page=1>.

Clements, Ron, Dir. Aladdin. Disney: 1992, Film. <http://www.imdb.com/ title/tt0103639/>.

Conaway, Carrie. "A Psychologic Effect of Stereotypes." Regional Review (2005): 40, 41. Web. 18 May 2011. <http://www.bos.frb.org/economic/ nerr/rr2005/q1/section3c.pdf>.

Jhally, Sut, Dir. Reel Bad Arabs: How Hollywood Vilifies a People. Perf. Shaheen, Jack. Media Education Foundation: Film.

Persson, Anna, and Dara Musher-Eizenman. "College Students Attitudes Towards Blacks and

   Arabs Following a Terrorist Attack as a Function of Varying Levels of Media Exposure."

   Journal of

Applied Social Psychology. 35.9 (2005): 1879-1893. Print.

"Policy and Research." Motion Picture Association of America. Motion Picture Association of

   America, 2011. Web. 9 May 2011. <http://www.mpaa.org/policy>.

Shaheen, Jack. ABC News: Nightline. Interview by John Donvan. 10 Oct 2002. TV. 9 May

   2011

Tutt, Daniel. "Impact of Negative Media Images." Spirit is a Bone. 3 Apr. 2010. Web. 2 May

   2011. <spiritisabone.wordpress.com>.

Wingfield, Marvin. "Arab Stereotypes and American Educators." American-Arabs Anti-Dis-

   crimination Committee, Mar 1995. Web. 2 May 2011. <www.adc.org>.

Alex,

I think you make a good case why some depictions may be bad, but I don't see a lot of support for the argument that depictions now are mainly false or negative outside what is noted
by the Arab Communities. In other words, I don't see where the controversy is. A controversy
suggests that there is a debate, where some people are standing up for the status quo. Who
supports the depictions in the movie industry or says that the depictions are more accurate
than inaccurate or that they, like many depictions, are harmless drama (e.g., other depictions are understood to not represent the norm, such as the man as hyper-masculine and
the woman as always beautiful and feminine)? For those who argue against them, are the
arguments based on studies that show not IF the false depictions exist, but THAT they exist?

You have some good information here that can and should be supplemented to more accurately depict a controversy. Let me know if you have any questions.

Prof Ris

Alexandra C. Land

Professor Ris

English 102

19 May 2011

Arabs in the Media

"Oh, I come from a land, from a faraway place, where the caravan camels roam, where they cut off your ear if they don't like your face. It's Barbaric, but hey, it's home."

The opening lyrics to Disney's *Aladdin* transported the audience from the dark, cool, musty theater to the dry, open, magical land of the Middle East. *Aladdin* was the first animated Disney film that focused on the Arab culture. Just like filmmakers before them, Disney added magic carpets, belly dancers, and oppressive men to capture the essence of the Western-coined term of "Arab Land." With the film industry in the United States claiming a wide influence on society, these so called "Arab Land" portrayals are an important source for American ideas of the Arabic culture. Unfortunately though, the Western portrayal of the Arabic culture is erroneous; no, there have not been any magic carpets discovered. More seriously than just the fantasy of a magic carpet, the erroneous portrayal has cemented harmful stereotypes into the American society causing a fear towards Arab-Americans. Arab-Americans, the general society, and Hollywood are affected by the usage of negative Arabic stereotypes.

Arabs have been falsely depicted in American media since the 20th century creating stereotypes defining a culture. The common Arab image was inherited by America from British and French traders who traveled to the Middle East in the 1800's (Jhally). As Americans, "We took them, embellished them" (Jhally), into exotic stereotypes. Writers and storytellers added fantasies filled with dangerous adventures and beautiful women to the traders' tales. Today, common themes have developed as staples presented in Arab images. The Arab-American Anti-Discrimination Committee (ADC) compiled a list of common stereotypes used in the popular media such as camel jockeys and towel-heads, notions of

122

foreign activity like belly dancing or terrorism, and descriptions of negative personifica-tion like greedy, dirty, uneducated, and violent. Other common stereotypes include the "oil sheik" with a thick accent donning a turban, a faceless woman suppressed by a veil, and incompetent terrorists plotting to undermine the United States and its allies. And what about the Arabic heroes? They have Anglo-Saxon features, lighter skin than the "bad guys," and an American accent (Wingfield).

Although the list is a compilation of stereotypes deemed negative by the ACD, the film writers and television program producers are using true depictions of Arab culture as a base. In one example, depicting veiled women is a common image shown in television broadcasts that has gained controversy. The association of the veil with Arab women stems from the roots of the Islamic religion in the Middle East. In surah 33, verse 59 of the Quran, the Holy Book of the Muslims, it states that women should dress modestly (Brahmachari). Within the religion, there are different levels of severity that each family chooses to follow which has led to the variety of garments used to veil women. No matter what garment the woman is wearing, in most cases, by wearing the veil, the woman is showing her will-ing submission to God and a closer connection to Mohammad (Brahmachari). Instead of representing this as being a symbol of religion, however, in the same way Western religions may expect their believers to dress in particular ways (such as Amish, Jewish Orthodox, and other groups), Western popular culture often do not represent this reason but only represents the veil as oppressive. This lack of information, along with presenting common stereotypes, are not uncommon in popular media.

Americans are exposed to high levels of popular media influence daily through common outlets such as film and television. With the American film industry contribut-ing "more than $180 billion annually to the U.S. economy" ("Policy and Research"), it has a heavy influence on how the American society will determine what is socially accept-able. Also, Americans spend more time watching television and going to movies than ever before. After the U.S. Census Bureau released the 2007 Statistical Abstract of the United

States, experts found staggering reports in the amount of media exposure adolescents and elementary children are receiving. The document reported that an "average youth 8 to 18 years old spends almost seven hours every day plugged in to the media" (Beg). The report includes types of media such as the Internet, film, television, video games, and popular literature such as magazines. With such a wide variety of media bombarding adolescents with different images and messages, it is easy to absorb and accept the media's content quickly rather than spend time processing the value of the content. So, at a time period where adolescents are beginning to explore their environment outside of the household, they are being exposed to violent images of different cultures—the Arab culture being one of them—that tamper with logical judgment.

The influence of American media allows for negative stereotyping of Arab Americans to become normal in societal thinking. Coupled with the large amount of time people are exposed to the media, the media's impact on the ideas of society can be explained by the accessibility principle. The accessibility principle states that people make social judgments "based on the information that come to the mind most readily [and] the more frequently a construct [image] is activated, the more accessible it becomes" (Persson & Musher-Eizenman). Because the "bad Arab" image is so commonplace in America, most people do not notice how frequently, and inappropriately, it is used, but in reality, "more than 300 movies, nearly 25 percent of all Hollywood movies" (Jhally), degrade the Arab culture by regurgitating the Western-born stereotypes. When the media constantly portrays the Arab culture negatively, the average person will be more likely to produce the same negative connotation first rather than a more factual depiction.

Recent historical events (Palestine/Israeli Conflict, Arab oil embargo, the Iranian Revolution, and 9/11), some would argue, are responsible for the anti-Arabic views in the media. Not all reactions are that simple, however. In an article by blogger Daniel Tutt, Tutt shares the research from Gordon Allport on the psychological aspects of stereotypes.

Gordon Allport is an American-born psychologist who founded the idea of trait theory of personality. Allport found that stereotypes are used to respond to inner anxieties towards "out-groups" (Tutt), in this case Arab-Americans. An out-group is the group that is outside a person's societal norm of interaction. People will naturally revert to stereotypes to cope with confrontation of an out-group. If the stereotypes that come readily to mind are negative, such as in the case of the Arab culture, a person is more likely to consider that group sub-human and express feelings of hate, dislike, fear, or other undesirable feelings. Jack Shaheen, an activist against vilifying the Arabic culture in the media, commented that, "Words such as Arab and Muslim are perceived as threatening words. . . . The stereotype has become . . . invisible to people [because] we've grown up with these images" (Jhally). By combining the theory of the accessibility principle with Allport's ideas on stereotypes, it is clear how Islamaphobia has emerged as a new social fear in non-Arab American cultures. Although social scientists do not have a clear definition of this new fear, the common concept consists of a fear towards those who practice Islam and individuals commonly associated with the Middle East.

After the attack on the World Trade Center in 2001, hate crimes and other physical discrimination tactics have been used on Arab Americans. The ADC reported that over 700 hate crimes were documented in the weeks that followed 9/11 (American-Arab Anti-Discrimination Research Institute 12). Although reports of hate crimes have decreased since the initial year after the terrorist attack, levels of violent discrimination are still significantly higher than pre-9/11 levels (American-Arab Anti-Discrimination Research Institute 12). The ADC also continues to report that most cases of violence towards the Arab Americans did not start as an intention of harm, but rather as isolated altercations. These altercations then escalated into ones in which racial stereotypes and slurs against Arab-Americans were used (American-Arab Anti-Discrimination Research Institute 12, 13).

Other kinds of communication seemed to fuel the fire of anti-Arabic sentiment. Politicians' statements might have done this: George W. Bush's statements immediately following the attack on 9/11 can be interpreted as a call to action; he noted that "Terrorism against our nation will not stand," and "Our enemies have made the mistake that America's enemies always make. They saw liberty and thought they saw weakness. And now, they see defeat" ("September 11 Quotes"). Statements like these might spur-on negative and unlawful behavior in times of emotional unrest. Also, instead of reducing the stereotypical roles of Arabs in movies to subdue cultural tensions, Hollywood actually produced "scores of films . . . that are clearly 'post-9/11 movies' in the sense that they encode and attempt to manage anxieties and concerns that are directly connected to the emotions and affects the attacks generated in American minds" (American-Arab Anti-Discrimination Research Institute 77). Hollywood has combined the established stereotypes of "Arab Land" of pre-9/11 with the anxiety and fear birthed from the terrorist attack on 9/11 to produce even more films that falsely depict the Arab culture. By doing this, the film industry is indirectly approving a fear based on inaccurate stereotypes.

Using negative stereotypes of the Arab culture influences the mindset and self-esteem of Arab-Americans as well. The ADC found that Arab-American children tend to feel inferior or ashamed of their culture due to the lack of education devoted towards their culture in school, the stereotypes depicted as humorous, and bullying. Carrie Conaway studied the psychological effects of stereotypes. She found that a person's performance is dependent on the stereotypical norm of the activity. If Arab-American children are constantly exposed to images degrading their culture or only images of Anglo-Saxon heroes, it can be theorized that the Arab-American children will feel inadequate, leading to a lack of achievement. (Conaway 40). This lack of achievement will only not affect the Arab-American community, but it will also affect society as a whole since it may contribute to higher unemployment rates or less contribution in a variety of fields.

Why would the media industry continue to use negative Arabic stereotypes if they clearly cause psychic and mental distress for Arab Americans and a recipe for an unbalanced society? For a profit. Hollywood continues to vilify Arabs in film because society has accepted the negative stereotypes. Hollywood has had a long track of degrading the popular out-group of the era. African Americans, Jews, and Catholics have all been negatively portrayed in film. In today's society, with Islamaphobia rising rapidly after 9/11, depicting Arabs as the "new" villain is psychologically accepted: "There's not going to be any pressure on any producer who makes a film vilifying Arabs. . . . There's a double standard . . . . . Hollywood is sort of clinging to this stereotype" (Shaheen). The intent of any business is to make a profit. In the film industry, making a profit means playing on the emotions of the audience to believe a story. In modern America, especial the twenty-first century, the general society is willing to accept an Arab as a villain. For film makers, it is too enticing to use the pre-packaged villain of the Arab; it's easier than fighting the protest from the audience that would occur if, for example, a Jewish American was depicted in similarly problematic ways.

Not all representations are aimed at isolating one culture to represent stereotypes. Aside from using cultural references as a basis for Arab stereotypes, many popular television programs use stereotypes from a wide variety of cultures and social groups. Additionally, some shows seem to draw from different cultural stereotypes to create humor, identify characters, and, at a deeper level, expose society's prejudices. One well-known series, *Family Guy*, is an excellent example of popular media using stereotypes in this way. The animated television show has portrayed every relevant stereotype in the series, including Arab culture, to show the problems of American society rather than to undermine any particular culture. In fact, Seth McFarlane, creator of Fox's hit, says that "[The producers'] philosophy [on Family Guy] was that we were the equal opportunity offender" (Epstein); in other words, no stereotype is off-limits because no culture is without some level of unacceptability in the general culture. Unfortunately, not enough media representations expose stereotypes in this manner.

The media in the United States has influenced the general society to believe in negative Arabic stereotypes. Even though Hollywood could potential suffer monetarily by withholding these negative stereotypes, society, as a whole, would profit. The general society will no longer be subject to degrading images that could influence harmful behavior. Meanwhile, the Arab-Americans would see a decrease in the overall discrimination rate. The American society would see *a whole new world* (Aladdin).

Works Cited

Aladdin. Dir. Ron Clements. Disney, 1992. Film. <http://www.imdb.com/title/tt0103639/>.

American-Arab Anti-Discrimination Research Institute. *Report on Hate Crimes and Discrimination Against American Arabs: 2003 and 2007*. (2008). 12,13,77. Web. 17 May 2011. <http://www.adc.org/PDF/hcr07.pdf>.

Beg, Sami. "Mass Media Exposure." *ABC News: Health* 15 Dec 2006. Web. 18 May 2011. <http://abcnews.go.com/Health/story?id=2727587&page=1>.

Brahmachari, Radhasyam. "The Origin of Veiling the Women in Islam and its Present Role." Islam Watch. 16 Sept 2008. Web. 1 June 2011. <http://www.islam-watch.org/Brahmachari/Origin-of-Veiling-in-Islam.htm>

Conaway, Carrie. "A Psychological Effect of Stereotypes." *Regional Review* (2005): 40-41. Web. 18 May 2011. http://www.bos.frb.org/economic/nerr/rr2005/q1/section3c.pdf

Epstein, Scott. Interview with Seth MacFarlane. Web 6 June 2011. <http://www.ugo.com/Channels/filmTv/features/familyguy/sethmacfarlane.asp>.

Jhally, Sut, Dir. *Reel Bad Arabs: How Hollywood Vilifies a People*. Perf. Jack Shaheen. Media Education Foundation: Film.

Persson, Anna and Dara Musher-Eizenman. "College Students Attitudes Towards Blacks and Arabs Following a Terrorist Attack as a Function of Varying Levels of Media Exposure." *Journal of Applied Social Psychology*. 35.9 (2005): 1879-1893. Print.

"Policy and Research." *Motion Picture Association of America*. Motion Picture Association of America, 2011. Web. 9 May 2011. <http://www.mpaa.org/policy>.

"September 11 Quotes." Wordpress. WordPress, 06 Sept 2006. Web. 6 June 2011. <http://quotes.wordpress.com/2006/09/06/september-11-quotes-9-11-quotes-911-quotes/>.

Land 9

Shaheen, Jack. *ABC News: Nightline*. Interview by John Donvan. 10 Oct 2002. TV. 9 May 2011

Tutt, Daniel. "Impact of Negative Media Images." *Spirit is a Bone*. 3 Apr. 2010. Web. 2 May 2011. <spiritisabone.wordpress.com>.

Wingfield, Marvin. "Arab Stereotypes and American Educators." *ADC*. American-Arabs Anti-Discrimination Committee, Mar 1995. Web. 2 May 2011. <www.adc.org>.

Example Student Writing   Plikerd 1

Laura Plikerd

English Composition 102

Cynthia Ris

Research Draft

Genetic Modification and the Issue of World Hunger

Behind the fruitfulness are men of understanding and knowledge and skill,

men who experiment with seed, endlessly developing the techniques for

greater crops of plants whose roots will resist the million enemies of the

earth: the molds, the insects, the rusts, the blights. These men work carefully

and endlessly to perfect the seed…"

~ *John Steinbeck, Grapes of* Wrath

Agriculture practices are always adapting to weather climates, populations changes, and technology. The most recent transformation in agriculture technology is genetically modifying organisms, creating GMO's or GM's foods. Since its creation, GM foods have been under debate. Are GM food's dangerous? Do they cause allergies? Will they destroy local environments? These questions and more are constantly being debated whenever the topic of GM food is brought up. Yet the idea that GM food will be able to solve world hunger keeps them constantly in the spot light. However, because of social and economical issues, GM foods are not capable of solving World Hunger.

Agricultural Practices are always changing by adapting to environmental issues and utilizing the latest technology. "Cultural agricultural practices change all the time", this is simply the natural order of the world

End quote? Who is Stone? Be sure to use signal phrases.

(Stone). Humans have developed from hunters/ gathers, into farmers/har-vesters. Agricultural tools have developed from shovels and hoes into giant tractors. Not only have humans and tools have developed over time, seeds have changed as well. The genetic engineering of seeds is not a new con-cept, "For centuries, farmers all over the world have been improving plant varieties" through breeding and crossbreeding select plants to achieve a bet-ter quality specimen that will have certain traits, like resistance to drought, fungi, and insects (Perriere). Yet modern technology has created ways for scientists to alter plant genetics to create new and "improved" organisms.

There are different types of Genetically Modifying Organisms tissue culture, Anther culture, and Gene marker selection. Tissue Culture is when a scien-tist grows a whole plant from a single cell or plant culture in a laboratory, without using a seed. Anther culture is a specific type of tissue culture using the anther of a plant, the part containing the male cell for reproduction and crossbreeding it for desired traits. The third type of genetically modifying plants is Gene marker selection, where specific genes with specific traits are linked to other plants DNA (Webner). This last type of genetic alteration is the one that causes the most controversy. Its with this new technology that science can create seeds that have genetic combinations not found any-where in nature.

The theory behind GMO's is that modern science can build upon a plants natural DNA to create a new organism that can be more easily grown, yet in actual practice the process is much more complicated. In theory, GMO's promise to change the world of agriculture. Through select genetic alteration scientists will be able to create super crops that are resil-ient to pesticides, insects, fungus, and have a higher yield of produce. These super seeds would be distributed to areas of the world that are suffering,

Check punctuation

So were these changes also genetic modification? If so, this may be important to note and to use perhaps as a more clear topic sentence for this paragraph. I'd suggest s new one beginning with the next paragraph. What do you want to say about modern-day techniques?

In addition to stating this, let your reader know through the topic sentence why this is relevant. Other-wise, it's unclear why your reader should pay attention to these three types of organisms. You may also reconsider how much of this detail you need.

Unclear movement between these two paragraphs

thus solving their agriculture problems. Yet, this is only in theory. A major

problem about the production of GMO's is the cost. These super seeds

are not cheap to produce. There is a long process in creating each seed,

which includes scientists working in laboratories, testing and manipulating

the seeds genetics. An everyday farmer cannot afford to alter seeds genet-

ics this way. This leaves large corporations and the government in charge

of this technology. It doesn't help that "Almost every step in the process

of genetic engineering has been patented by agribusiness" companies

(Webner). There have been multiple seeds developed for specific diseases

in third world countries. For example " in Africa, a parasitic weed of the

genus *Striga* inserts a sort of underground hypodermic needle into the roots

of the corn and sorghum, sucking off water and nutrients" (Webner). Only

large private foundations, like the Gates and Rockefeller Foundations, have

enough money to actually buy these seeds and send them to the third world

countries that they are needed in. There is a big problem when farmers

can no longer afford to buy seeds in which to farm with. This also disturbs

many traditional customs when it comes to seeds. Many farmers save seeds

from their current selection in order to plant them the next year. Yet with

genetically modified seeds, farmers would be forced to buy seeds each year,

whether they had a good harvest or not the previous growing season (Perri-

ere). This is something that many farmers just cannot afford to do, "because

they often have to borrow money to buy more expensive GM seeds. If their

crops fail, particularly repeatedly, they can find themselves unable to repay

the loans" (Goering). In India there has been as increased rate of suicide by

farmers who have fallen into debt and have no way to repay their loans. The

gap between the companies that produce GM foods and the rural farmer

makes affording GMO's almost impossible.

Source needed for these specific points.

Unclear if affordability is the entire point of this paragraph. If it is, can you further divide your discussion into more discreet concerns about affordability so as to focus your points along with clearer topic sentences?

133

One company in particular, Monsanto, has taken over the GMO market and become the poster child for genetically modified organisms. Monsanto is a large company based in St Louis, Missouri, in fact this one company "represents 55 percent of the world's GE crops"(Leahy). Monsanto started becoming interested in GMO's in 1997 when they began trying to produce seeds that were genetically engineered to withstand their weed killing, Roundup. The idea behind this is that farmers could plant seeds closer together and spray the entire lot with roundup, killing only the weeds, because the seeds could grow regardless of the chemical exposure. Yet something not commonly known is that Roundup is "sold as a harmless biodegradable weed killer, [yet] it is a form of Agent Orange, and as we know all too well from Vietnam, it causes cancers, extreme birth defects, and many other problems leading to illness and eventual death"(Robin). This product is something that is highly dangerous, yet Monsanto has us spraying in on our food.

What's the main point of this paragraph? Additionally, what is the "it" that is referred to in your quote? Agent Orange? Roundup? How does it cause eventual death? From spraying it on our food? Unclear.

The debate over the safety of GMO's has made it hard for them to be introduced to foreign countries. The first genetically engineered product that Monsanto released was the "Bovine Growth Hormone for boosting milk production, [which] was introduced in 1994 to a furious debate over whether it was disastrous to health" (Langreth). The problem is that Bovine Growth Hormone "rBGH is a mutation of a cow's growth hormone which greatly speeds up the animal's milk production. According to some medical experts, rBGH also increases the amount of blood IGF-1 levels in consumers, increasing their risk of cancer"(Jefferys). It doesn't help that in the past Monsanto has acted the part of a "bully" "to get new products approved Monsanto uses political and financial pressure to force them through regulatory bodies, When problems occur the company allegedly uses intimidation against people who complain"(Jefferys). In fact the George W. Bush ad-

ministration "filed a [law] suit at the World Trade Organization (WTO) to

force Europe to lift its moratorium on GE foods. In a press release, CropLife

America commended the US decision saying 'the EU's illegal moratorium

had a negative ripple effect of creeping regulations which have resulted in

denying food to starving people '" (Mittal). At the same time products con-

taining rBGH milk have made their way into Europe and Canada through

US manufactured milk products. This has happened because "Monsanto has

waged a tough campaign in the US making a label revealing the presence

of rBGH illegal" (Jefferys). In fact farmers can be hit with lawsuits if they

try to label their products, both admitting to their milk containing rBGH

or claiming to be rBGH free. Many governments around the world, "led

by the United States, maintain that GE foods and crops are 'substantially

equivalent' to conventional foods, and therefore require neither mandatory

labeling nor premarket safety testing" (Webner). The fact is at this point in

time we don't know what the long term effects of GMO's are, yet the are be-

ing pushed into are food supply without anyway for the consumer to know

that they are even there. While the United States government has openly

accepted GM food, other countries are a lot more reluctant to accept the

"Frankenfoods". With the long-term health effects being unknown, industry

and governments are preventing the labeling of GM food products because

they know that "If they were labeled, no one would buy them"(Leahy).

Many countries have been very skeptical of GMO's and have been

hesitant to introduce them to their ecosystems. One example of a coun-

try standing up against GM food is Zambia. In 2002 " Zambia was bold

enough to refuse the US offer of money to buy food because the US insisted

that it only had the GM variety to offer" (Madeley). The United States was

> I'll stop here, but note the string of quotes you use to tell your story for you. (Highlight in your own paper what your quotes are, and you'll see how you're letting the quotes do your work for you throughout the paper). You need to identify for each paragraph what your main concern is and then support it with facts, data, statistics, expert opinion, etc., not with a string of quotes.

furious that a country that was experiencing such turmoil would reject their offer, yet there is no shortage of non-GM food that could have been offered to Zambia. What is interesting to note is "The US aid agency, USAID, receives some of its funds from Monsanto" and in turn "almost 80 percent of USAID contracts go directly to US firms" (Madeley). Zambia is not the only country that is against GM foods, Europe has been one of the strongest opponents of GM foods. In fact "in June 1999, the environmental ministers of the European Union imposed a moratorium on the commercialization of new varieties of GMO's" (Perriere). While Europe still opposes GM foods, they are still being brought over in food products produced in the Unites States, a country that refuses to label them as genetically modified. Also a lot of Indian farmers openly oppose GMO's. Vandana Shiva is an Indian social activist and "one of the world's largest opponents of GM crops" (Stone). Shiva is extremely against GM crops and insists that they are not needed; instead she promotes small-scale farming.

Notice that this paragraph could be more concise if you avoid the string of quotes approach. Many countries have refused the offer of GM foods. These countries include . . . . The main reasons seem to be . . . . (if there are main reasons—I don't realy see that and so I'm not sure the point other than that countries are refusing this—not a bad point to make, but not one that needs this much space).

The major issue with World Hunger is not that there isn't enough food for the planet's population, but the distribution of the worlds food supply is not even. In India, "some 260 million people live below the poverty line" and "villagers in states like Rajasthan are eating bark off trees to stay alive", yet they have "become the world's second largest rice exporter"(Madeley). In fact "with 80 million tonnes of excess food grains, the government of Indian was unable to find enough export markets" (Mittal). There are "children in Argentina dropping dead at the same time as maize, meat, soy, and wheat is exported from the country's fertile land" (Madeley). The problem is "over a third of the grain grown in the developing world is destined for livestock, which in turn is eaten by consumers in wealthy countries. It is not a shortage of food production, but poverty that keeps people hungry" (Mittal). Even though companies like Monsanto claim to want to produce more food for farmers to end world hunger, it isn't the lack of food that is keeping people starving. It has been shown that "global trade in food has destroyed the ability of farmers to grow food for their families and communities" (Mittal). Also with the rise of ethanol has caused the price of corn to rise, making it harder for families in developing countries to afford to pay corn for food.

What is the main point of this paragraph?

If there is going to be a solution for world hunger, the changes need to start in the first world countries. Companies, like Monsanto, are not out to solve world hunger; they are using this plight as a way to involve people's emotion, and to ultimately to make money. The general population needs

Appropriate term? What do you mean by this?

to be more informed about the crisis happening everyday with every bit of food that if eaten. While genetic engineering may be the future of food, there needs to be a better reason than solving world hunger, because producing more food for first world countries is not a solution. Food needs to stay in the communities it is produced in. Small-scale farmers have proven to be more productive with their land than large corporations because they are more invested with both time and money in the food that is produced. Countries like the United States need to take more responsibility in the crisis of world hunger. We need to get back to growing our own food locally and not importing from countries that need to keep their food for themselves. The United States is a giant country with a wide range of terrains and climates. We need to utilize what we have and make the most of it. Only time will be able to tell if we will be able to end world hunger, but the changes need to start now.

Have you shown this or is this a red herring? What is the main "change [that needs] to start"? Take a paragraph for each way we need to start with supported evidence for each (i.e., an indication of who other than you is claiming that this is what needs to be done) .

"There is a crime here that goes beyond denunciation. There is a sorrow here that weeping cannot symbolize. There is a failure here that topples all

our success. The fertile earth, the straight tree rows, the sturdy trunks, and

the ripe fruit. And children dying of pellagra must die because a profit can-

not be taken from an orange. And coroners must fill in the certificates—died

of malnutrition---because the food must rot, must be forced to rot."

John Steinbeck, Grapes of Wrath

Laura,
The length of the paper is a bit misleading. I mentioned in class that one problem writers sometimes have is allowing quotes to speak for them; this is what's happening here. A major problem with that is when there is not accompanying analysis that clearly states what the main concern is that is being addressed by the quotes, is that paragraphs get unfocused, main points are left unstated, and specific evidence is sometimes lacking. See my marginal comments and be sure that you are using topic sentences to state the claims you are making, that each follows logically from the paragraph before, and that you are using your analysis in conjunction with a variety of support to build your claims.

Cynthia Ris

Works Cited

Barboza, David. "Cornering the market on gene-altered seeds; Monsanto's pricing tactics under fire." *New York Times* 9 Jan. 2004: News. pg. 1. Print.

Charles, Daniel. *Lords of the Harvest: Biotech, Bio Money, and the Future of Food.* Cambridge, Massachusetts: Perseus Publishing, 2001. Print.

Evenson R.E, V. Santaniello. *Economic and Social Issues in Agricultural Biotechnology.* NY: CABI Publishing, 2002. Print.

Jefferys, Daniel. "GM protestor at yesterday's case, the record that shames the Biotech Bully Boys." *Daily Mail (London)* 18 Feb 1999: 8. Print.

LaGesse, David. "Monsanto's Biotech Makeover Takes Root." *Us and News World Report* 27. Aug. 2007: n. pag. Web. 26 Oct 2010.

Langreth Robert, , Herper, Matthew. "The Planer vs. Monsanto." *Forbes* 1/18/2010: 64-69. Web. 26 Oct 2010.

Leahy, Stephen. "Environment: Biotech Crops haven't exactly changed the world." *Global Information Network* (2006): n. pag. Web. 26 Oct 2010.

Madeley, John. "GM food aid? No thanks." *Appropriate Technology* 30.1 2003. n. pag. Web. Research Library. March 2003. Retrieved at Langsom Library.

Mittal, Anuradna. "Pretending to help the Poor." *Alternatives Journal* 29.4 (2003): n. pag. Web. 26 Oct 2010.

Perriere, Robert Ali Brac de la, Severet, Frank. *Brave New Seeds, The threat of GM crops to farmers.* NY: St. Martin's Press Inc, 2000. Print.

Robin, Marie- Monique. "The World according to Monsanto." *National Film Board of Canada* 2008: n. pag. Web. 26 Oct 2010.

Serageldin I. , Persley, G.J. *Biotechnology and Sustainable Development, Voices of the North and South.* Cambridge, MA: CABI Publishing in association with Bibliotheca Alexandrina, 2003. Print.

Smith, James. "Globalizing Vulnerability: The Impact of unfair Trade on Developing Country Agriculture." n. pag. Web. 26 Oct 2010.

Stone, Glenn Davis. "Biotechnology and Political Ecology of Information in India." *Human Organization* 63.2 (2004): 127. Web. 26 Oct 2010.

Webner, Karl. *Food Inc. How Industrial Food is Making us Sicker, Fatter, and Poorer- and what you can do about it.* NY: Public Affairs, 2009. Print.

Weissman, Robert. "Grim Day for Monsanto." *Multinational Monitar* 25.6 2004. n. pag. Web. *Research Library.*

Laura Plikerd

English Composition 102

Cynthia Ris

Research Paper

Genetic Modification and the Issue of World Hunger

Behind the fruitfulness are men of understanding and knowledge and skill, men who experiment with seed, endlessly developing the techniques for greater crops of plants whose roots will resist the million enemies of the earth: the molds, the insects, the rusts, the blights. These men work carefully and endlessly to perfect the seed. . . .

~ John Steinbeck, Grapes of Wrath

Agriculture practices are always adapting to weather climates, populations changes, and technology. The most recent transformation in agriculture technology is genetically modifying organisms (GMOs) or producing genetically modified (GM) foods. Since its creation, GM foods have been under debate. Are GM food's dangerous? Do they cause allergies? Will they destroy local environments? These questions and more are constantly being debated whenever the topic of GM food is brought up. Yet the idea that GM food will be able to solve world hunger keeps them constantly in the spot light. However, because of social and economical issues, GM foods are not capable of solving world hunger.

A plant's genetics can be altered in different ways, some of which are natural and some of which use modern science and are more controversial. Genetic engineering of seeds is not a new concept; "for centuries, farmers all over the world have been improving plant varieties" through breeding and crossbreeding select plants to achieve a better quality specimen that will have certain traits, like resistance to drought, fungi, and insects (Perriere and Severet 8). While this is still genetic engineering, it is a natural process that is limited in its abilities. Yet modern technology has created ways for scientists to alter plant genetics to create new and "improved" organisms. The different types of GMOs are tissue culture,

140

anther culture, and gene marker selection. Tissue culture is when a scientist grows a whole plant from a single cell or plant culture in a laboratory without using a seed. Anther culture is a specific type of tissue culture using the anther of a plant, the part containing the male cell for reproduction, and crossbreeding it for desired traits. The third type of genetically modifying plants is gene marker selection, where specific genes with specific traits are linked to other plants DNA (Webner 68-69). This last type of genetic alteration is the one that causes the most controversy. With this new technology, science can create seeds that have genetic combinations not found anywhere in nature.

In theory, GMOs promise to change the world of agriculture; through select genetic alteration, scientists will be able to create super crops that are resilient to pesticides, insects, and fungus and also have a higher yield of produce. These super seeds would be distributed to areas of the world that are suffering, thus solving their agriculture problems (Serageldin and Persley 22). There have been multiple seeds developed for specific ailments that effect third world countries. For example, " in Africa, a parasitic weed of the genus *Striga* inserts a sort of underground hypodermic needle into the roots of the corn and sorghum, sucking off water and nutrients" (Webner 73). A seed resistant to Striga was one of those super seeds that were developed; however, even though one hundred million people lose a large part of their crops to *Striga*, the super seed never made it to Africa because the farmers there could not afford to buy it. These super seeds have the potential to grow in extreme conditions and produce high yields of crops. In reality, though, it is hard for these seeds to affect the areas of the world where they are needed.

The high cost of GMOs prevents them from reaching the people that require them the most. These super seeds are not inexpensive to produce (LaGesse 6). There is a long process in creating each seed, which includes scientists working in laboratories where they test and manipulate the seeds genetics. It can take three to six years to create a new type of plant, and even if the plant makes it to that phase in its testing, it still has to undergo safety inspections and be analyzed in a laboratory (LaGesse 6). The everyday farmer cannot afford to alter seeds genetics this way. This leaves large corporations and the government in charge of this technology. Only large private foundations, like the Bill and Melinda Gates Foundation and Rockefeller Foundation, have enough money to actually buy these seeds and send them to the third world countries where they are needed.

Even if the seeds can get to the countries, the introduction of GM seeds into the environment may disrupt the cultural traditions in agricultural societies. Many farmers save seeds from their current selection in order to plant them the next year. In many cases, "80 per cent of the seeds used in the Third World still come from the preceding harvest" (Perriere and Severet 28). Yet with GM seeds, farmers would be forced to buy seeds each year, whether they had a good harvest or not the previous growing season (Perriere and Severet12). This is something that many farmers just cannot afford to do, "because they often have to borrow money to buy more expensive GM seeds. If their crops fail, particularly repeatedly, they can find themselves unable to repay the loans" (Goering). In India there has been as increased rate of suicide by farmers who have fallen into debt and have no way to repay the loans they received from banks. The companies that make GM seeds are interested in making a product that sells so they can make money; they are not necessarily interested in the needs of the famers that use their products. They are companies and therefore need to make profits in order to pay for their research and to please investors. Farmers rely on seeds for their livelihood; it could be argued that alterations made to those seeds should be made to benefit the farmer, not the company.

One company in particular, Monsanto, has taken over the GMO market and has become the poster child for GMOs. Monsanto, a large company based in St Louis, Missouri, "represents 55 percent of the world's GE [genetically engineered] crops"(Leahy 1). David LaGesse, from *U.S. News and World Report*, writes that Monsanto was once a company that mainly focused on industrial chemicals, but Monsanto is now almost completely focused on plant breeding (LaGesse 2). Monsanto's "giant" status can be credited to the fact that the company spent a lot of time and money in the 80's and 90's buying up small seed companies (LaGesse 5). Because of its large size, a lot of GM food's can be credited or connected to Monsanto.

Since their introduction to the market, it has been debated whether or not it is safe to consume GMO's. The first genetically engineered product that Monsanto released was the "Bovine Growth Hormone for boosting milk production, [which] was introduced in 1994 to a furious debate over whether it was disastrous to health," says Robert Langreth and Matthew Herper, writers for *Forbes* magazine (5). The Bovine Growth Hormone speeds up milk production so a farmer can have fewer cows but still produce a large amount of milk. Bovine Growth Hormone was introduced to the market without satisfying safety testing. Since then some studies have shown that it can cause increased amount to blood levels in consumers, an increased risk of getting cancer, and early onset of puberty (Jefferys 2). Because the long-term effect of GMOs is uncertain, many people would like more safety testing on these products before they are introduced to the market.

There is an ongoing controversy regarding whether GM foods should have to carry a label expressing that they have been genetically modified. This has led many people to be skeptical over the safety of these products. Many governments around the world, "led by the United States, maintain that GE foods and crops are 'substantially equivalent' to conventional foods, and therefore require neither mandatory labeling nor premarket safety testing" (Webner 80). Many people have begun to question why the government refuses to label the foods that have been genetically modified. Some have come to the conclusion that the government and the big business that make GMOs, companies like Monsanto, have purposely created laws with such ambiguous terms that GMOs don't actually qualify as foods—this way they don't require the same amount of testing. The film *The World According to Monsanto/ Le Monde Selon Monsanto* a film sponsored by the National Film Board of Canada, goes in depth and documents how Monsanto has worked within the political system to make their ideals FDA policies (Robin 1). The fact is, at this point in time, we don't know what the long term effects of GMOs are, yet they are being pushed into are food supply without any way for the consumer to know that they are even there. While the United States government has openly accepted GM food, other countries are much more reluctant to accept the "Frankenfoods." With the long-term health effects being unknown, the large food industry and the United States government are preventing the labeling of GM food products because, some claim, they know that "If they were labeled, no one would buy them" (Leahy 2).

Many countries have been very skeptical of GMOs and have been hesitant to introduce them to their ecosystems. Europe has been one of the strongest opponents of GM foods. In fact, "in June 1999, the environmental ministers of the European Union imposed a moratorium on the commercialization of new varieties of GMOs" (Perriere and Severet 84). While Europe still opposes GM foods, they are still being brought over in food products produced in the Unites States, a country that refuses to label them as genetically modified. Many African countries have banned the use of GM foods. In fact, in 2002, "Zambia was bold enough to refuse the US offer of money to buy food because the US insisted that it only had the GM variety to offer," says John Madeley a writer for *Appropriate Technology* (Madeley 1). Indian farmers have strenuously opposed the introduction of GMOs into their ecosystem, partially to no avail. In India, Monsanto has introduced "Bollgard" cotton, a plant that has been modified with the Bt bacterium; this gene makes them fatal to some types of insects that try and eat them (Stone 128). All these countries fear that GM crops will have a negative effect on their local environment, causing super weeds and genetic pollution to the area.

Companies like Monsanto claim to want to produce more food for farmers to end world hunger, yet it isn't the lack of food that is keeping people starving. Many of the countries that produce the most food also happen to be countries with the most famished communities. In India, "some 260 million people live below the poverty line," yet at the same time they have become the world's second largest producer of rice (Madeley 1). There are also "children in Argentina dropping dead at the same time as maize, meat, soy, and wheat is exported from the country's fertile land" (Madeley 1). These countries that have the land and climate to produce large amounts of food are producing food in great quantities, but they just aren't keeping that food on their own soil.

The real problem is that "global trade in food has destroyed the ability of farmers to grow food for their families and communities" (Mittal 1). Instead of farmers keeping the food they produce in their own communities, they sell this food to the highest bidder and ship it all over the world—that is, if the food doesn't rot in a warehouse somewhere waiting to be shipped out. Anuradha Mittal, a writer for *Alternatives Journal*, summarizes this problem quite well: " It is not a shortage of food production, but poverty that keeps people hungry" (Mittal 1). The globalization of the market has really harmed countries that need to keep the food they produce within their own countries border.

The answer to world hunger does not lay in one solution; instead, there are many factors that cause world hunger that have to be addressed before a real change can be made. One way to start addressing the issue of world hunger would be to come up with alternative sources of energy. With the rise of ethanol, a lot of corn that would be going to feed families is now going into our fuel tanks. It has also affected what plants farmers have decided to plant. Instead of planting wheat and soy, farmers have begun to plant more corn, because they can sell it for more. This has lead to the increase in the prices of all grains, because there are less grains being produced (Pollan). Also, agriculture has become dependant on fossil fuels; food writer Michael Pollan notes that, "Today it takes 10 calories of fossil-fuel energy to produce one calorie of food energy." Solar energy is the greenest form of technology and would not only help get rid of our dependence on fossil fuels, but would help the environment in general by decreasing the harmful greenhouse admissions that are produced by fossil fuels when they burn ("Solar Energy"). If we could harness the energy of the sun, we would need less fossil fuel, including ethanol, and could get the corn that would be used in our vehicles into the mouths of the people.

The ultimate solution to end world hunger is sustainable agriculture. Sustainable agriculture is using natural resources available in the environment to farm in a way that does not cause damage to the ecosystem. Sustainable agriculture creates a relationship between the farmer, the consumer, and the environment. When people are in control of their own land, they put more effort in maintaining it; in fact, the University of Essex showed through one of the largest studies of sustainable agriculture that took into account over fifty-seven countries and 12.6 million famers, that when farmers switched to sustainable agriculture, their production rate increased by seventy nine percent (Webner 116-17). Not only will sustainable agriculture produce more food without using genetically modified organisms, but it will also help address multiple agriculture issues. Karl Webner, the author of *Food Inc.* suggests that "sustainable agriculture will have other beneficial ripples: addressing hunger and poverty, improving public health, and preserving biodiversity (Webner 166). Right now there is a growing movement, the slow food movement, which endorses sustainable agriculture. This movement, that started in Italy in 1986 in protest to McDonalds, has reached around the world and is active even in Ohio. A Cincinnati local, Julie Silber, is one of those people in the movement who is interested in growing food locally because of the chemicals that is in processed food. She feels that growing food locally and eating food while it is in season is the way to become less dependent on foreign food (Silber). Sustainable agriculture will benefit the plant and end world hunger at the same time.

GMOs are not the solution to world hunger, even if companies like Monsanto would like them to be. Countries dependent on agriculture as their main source of income cannot afford GMOs. Because of their high cost it is not practical to think that countries where a large part of the population is staving can afford to pay extra for seeds that have genetically modified. While companies like Monsanto are going to continue to produce GMOs, they need to come up with a better excuse than solving world hunger, because this is something they are not doing. When we adapt our current agricultural practices to the

changing times, and adopt ideas like renewable energy and sustainable agriculture, we will
be able to help start end world hunger.

"There is a crime here that goes beyond denunciation. There is a sorrow here that weeping
cannot symbolize. There is a failure here that topples all our success. The fertile earth, the
straight tree rows, the sturdy trunks, and the ripe fruit. And children dying of pellagra must
die because a profit cannot be taken from an orange. And coroners must fill in the certifi-
cates—died of malnutrition---because the food must rot, must be forced to rot."

~ John Steinbeck, Grapes of Wrath

Plikerd 9

Works Cited

Goering, Laurie. "Indian Activist Vandana Shiva says 'Relying on GM Food Crops is Suicidal.'" *Health Freedom Alliance.* March 22, 2010. Web. 8 Nov 2010.

Jefferys, Daniel. "GM protestor at yesterday's case, the record that shames the Biotech Bully Boys." *Daily Mail (London)* 18 Feb 1999: 8. Print.

LaGesse, David. "Monsanto's Biotech Makeover Takes Root." *Us and News World Report* 27. Aug. 2007: n. p. Web. 26 Oct 2010.

Langreth Robert and Matthew Herper. "The Planer vs. Monsanto." *Forbes* 18 Jan 2010: 64-69. Web. 26 Oct 2010.

Leahy, Stephen. "Environment: Biotech Crops haven't exactly changed the world." *Global Information Network* (2006): n. p. Web. 26 Oct 2010.

Madeley, John. "GM Food Aid? No thanks." *Appropriate Technology* 30.1 (2003): n. p. Web. *Research Library.* March 2003. Retrieved at Langsam Library.

Mittal, Anuradna. "Pretending to help the Poor." *Alternatives Journal* 29.4 (2003): n. p. Web. 26 Oct 2010.

Perriere, Robert Ali Brac de la and Frank Severet. *Brave New Seeds, The Threat of GM Crops to Farmers.* NY: St. Martin's Press Inc, 2000. Print.

Pollan, Michael. "How to Feed the World." *Michael Pollan.* Newsweek, 19/may/2008. Web. 8 Nov 2010. <http://michaelpollan.com/articles-archive/how-to-feed-the-world/>.

Robin, Marie-Monique. "The World According to Monsanto." *National Film Board of Canada* 2008: n. p. Web. 26 Oct 2010.

Serageldin I and G. J. Persley. *Biotechnology and Sustainable Development, Voices of the North and South.* Cambridge, MA: CABI Publishing in Association with Bibliotheca Alexandrina, 2003. Print.

Silber, Julie. Telephone Interview by Laura Plikerd. 09 Nov. 2010.

"Solar Energy Advantages Disadvantages." *facts-about-solar-energy.com.* Small Biz Web Solution, 2006. Web. 9 Nov 2010. <http://www.facts-about-solar-energy.com/solar-energy-advantages-disadvantages.html>.

Stone, Glenn Davis. "Biotechnology and Political Ecology of Information in India." *Human Organization* 63.2 (2004): 127. Web. 26 Oct 2010.

Webner, Karl. Food Inc. *How Industrial Food is Making Us Sicker, Fatter, and Poorer—and What You Can Do About It.* NY: Public Affairs, 2009. Print.

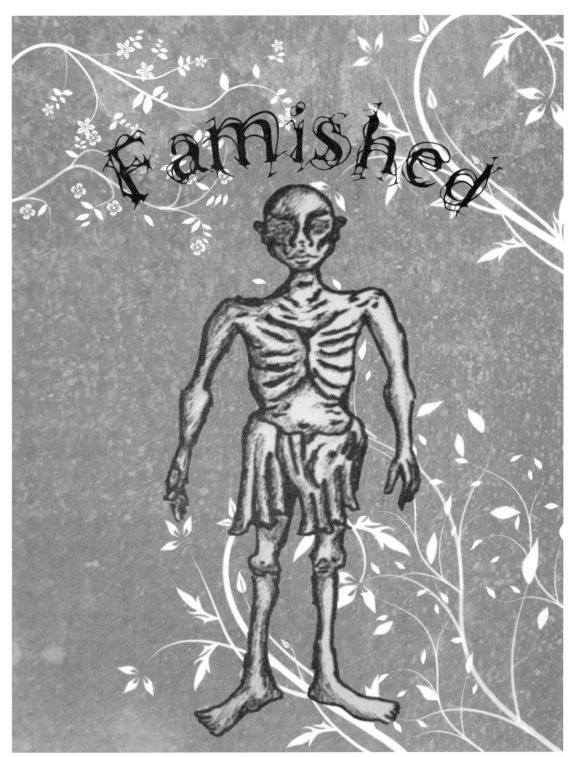

FAM·ISH

[FAM-ISH]

—VERB

1.

TO SUFFER OR CAUSE
TO SUFFER EXTREME
HUNGER; STARVE.

2.

TO STARVE TO DEATH.

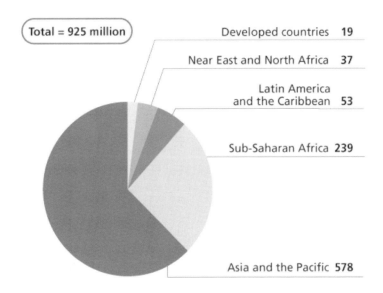

Total = 925 million

Developed countries **19**

Near East and North Africa **37**

Latin America
and the Caribbean **53**

Sub-Saharan Africa **239**

Asia and the Pacific **578**

Even though the exact number is unknown, it is estimated that there are 925 million people in the world suffering from malnutrition

1.2 Billion people live on less than 1 US dollar per day

In America...

Nearly 15 million children in the United States - 21% of all children - live in families with incomes below the federal poverty level

These children who are undernourished are at risk of developing a serious health, social, and/or educational problem

Feeding America, a nationwide program provides groceries for one in eight Americans

In 2008, 49.1 million Americans lived in food insecure households, 32.4 million adults and 16.7 million children.

In 2008, 4.1 percent of all U.S. households (4.8 million households) accessed emergency food from a food pantry one or more times.

Poverty is the principal cause of hunger. The causes of poverty include poor people's lack of resources, an extremely unequal income distribution in the world and within specific countries, conflict, and hunger itself.

and yet...

Hunger is also a cause of poverty. By causing poor health, low levels of energy, and even mental impairment, hunger can lead to even greater poverty by reducing people's ability to work and learn.

What can you do?
GET
INVOLVED!!!
THATS RIGHT, THE BEST
THING YOU CAN DO IS
GET INVOLVED WITH
YOUR COMMUNITY

Want to Volunteer? Try the FreeStore FoodBank

The Freestore Foodbank assits thousands of people everyday across 20 counties in Ohio, Kentucky, and Indiana, they provide over 12 million pounds of food to families each year.

Ways you can help-
Volunteer- (walk, work in the warehouse, greet people)
Advocate- (write to public officials, learn about hunger and poverty, stay informed)
Donate- (money, food, clothing, household items)

You can find out more information at
http://fsfbmedia.org/beta/

Want to get involved at the University of Cincinnati?

Try out Serve Beyond Cincinnati

"Serve Beyond Cincinnati is a University of Cincinnati student group that strives to do more than watch the world turn. We are completely organized by and comprised of college students who want to see real change. SBC engages UC students in multicultural world service experiences through participation in construction projects that increase quality of life."

If you are interested in donating money, there are lots of websites online offering to do different services in different areas of the world. Before donating you should do a little research on the company or organization to make sure it is real and not a scam.

One good organization to donate to is Kiva Loans

With Kiva loans you donate to individuals across the globe that are in need of supplies in order to run their own businesses. This can be anything from seeds, fertilizer, animals, or products of some sort. Because this is a loan, over a set period of time you receive your money back, from there you can choose to collect your funds or donate again.

As of November 2009, Kiva has facilitated over $100 million in loans.

Whats the Deal with GMO'S?

GMO's or GM foods are genetically modified organisms. There is a controversy surrounding GMO's, Are GM food's dangerous? Do they cause allergies? Will they destroy local environments? The one factor that keeps them in the spotlight however is 'can they solve world hunger?' The answer to this question is no, the main reason for this being the cost. GMO's are very expensive to produce, scientists spend a lot of time in labs trying different genetic combinations and then proceed to grow and test these plants. Companies, like Monsanto, then paten the rights to the genetic makeup they have created, charging farmers for the right to grow it. Even if the plants that have been genetically modified are resistant to some specific things, like a certain type of insect or weed killer, it does not guarantee a good harvest for the farmer. It also does not promise higher yields of the crop planted. The only one benefiting from this arrangement are the companies that produce the GM foods. Because of this economic issues, GMO's at this point in time are not able to solve world hunger.

Buy Local Food

Why?

Money stays within your own community

It is Beneficial to the environment because less fossils fuels are needs to transport the food, on average food in the super market travels 1,500 miles to get to the store while local food travels only about 57 miles

Fresh food tastes better

When?

Buying Produce when it is in season guarantees freshness

Where?

An easy way to find a local farmers market is to check online or at your local health food store. A good website to check out is http://www.localharvest.org/.

What Can You do to lessen Your Impact on the Enviroment?

Eat Less Meat- it takes 10 pounds of grain to produce one pound of beef. You don't have to give up meat completely, but try eating vegetarian meals at least once and week

Buy Local- Take an interest in how your food is being raised

Take Public Transit- If you are going somewhere locally, ride the bus or car pull

Ride a Bike or Walk- not only is it great exercise, it doesn't use any fossil fuels that are harmful to the environment

The best way to know where and how your food is grown is to grow it

yourself

Benefits of Gardening Include

Homegrown fruits and vegetables
Exercise
Stress Reduction
Provides a link to nature
Helps builds communities
Etcetera

Start Your Own Garden

First you need to decide where you want to grow your new garden. Evaluate the spaces available to you. Do you live in an apartment or house? Do you have excess to a large or small space? Indoor and outdoor gardens both have pros and cons. With an outdoor garden you have more space for you plants to grow, but at the same time your plants are at the mercy of the environment and can be harmed by both weather and insects. Indoor gardens are smaller and some plants do not yield produce indoors, but are usually easer to take care of and provide an excellent room decoration.

There are just a few things that every plant needs to grow, water, nutrients, and sunlight. Depending on what type of plant you are growing you will need different variations of those things. Its best to do some research on your seeds, you can use the instructions on the seed packet or do some re-search online or at the library. Every seed takes time to sprout after first planted, but be patient because with care you can have own garden.

A great resource on how to start an indoor garden out of kitchen items you usually through away is " Don't throw it, Grow it, 68 windowsill plants from kitchen scraps" by Deborah Peterson and Millicent Selsam

Source Notes for Recast Zine "Famished" by Laura Plikerd

Pictures were drawn by Laura Plikerd

Some information on GMOs was taken from the class research essay based on sources noted in that Works Cited.

Pages 153-54:
"925 Million Hungry People in 2010." Hunger Notes. 7 May 2010. Web. 9 Oct 2010. <http://www.worldhunger.org/articles/Learn/world%20 hunger%20facts%202002.htm>

Page 155:
United States. "Household Food Security in the United States, 2008." United States Department of Agriculture: Economic Research Service. 16 Nov 2009. Web. 10 Oct 2010. <http://www.ers.usda.gov/publica-tions/err83>

Page 159:
University of Cincinnati web site at <www.uc.edu>

Page 160:
For more on Kiva loans, see <www.kiva.org>

Page 163:
"Your Food... Buy Local." The World Women Want. 2010. Web. 2 Oct 2010. <http://www.theworldwomenwant.com/yourworld/food/local. php?page=bl>

Page 164:
Many sites, including:
"Offset Your Carbon Footprint." EnviroCitizen.org. 2008–2010. Web. 4 Oct 2010. <http://www.envirocitizen.org/carbonfootprints.html>

Example Student Writing

Taylor Smith

Professor Malek

English 102

Research Proposal

1 February 2012

Title: Standardized Tests: Every High School Student's Biggest Enemy

Introduction: Standardized Tests, such as the ACT and SAT have become a major contributor in a student's admission to a University. Colleges have used the scores as a major factor in choosing whether or not to admit the student to their school. Standardized test scores have driven a huge controversy among several different groups including universities, students, teachers, parents, minorities, etc. This paper will discuss why standardized tests should be overlooked in the admissions process, the effect these tests have on students and minority groups, the positives and negatives of dropping the tests from the admissions requirements, and alternative routes universities can take instead of relying on standardized tests.

Thesis: For universities the SAT and ACT is an easy, inexpensive, and accurate factor, yet to many students the SAT is an unfair representation of the student's gained knowledge and intellect. Standardized Test Scores, such as the ACT and SAT, should be eliminated from the college admission requirements because they do not predict a student's accurate performance in college as well as does their high school GPA; they discriminate against minorities, and they have a negative effect on students' admissions, especially when schools consider the tests as having more weight than overall high school performance.

Background: Standardized Tests were created to help colleges see how students perform based on a standardized level of knowledge. Since academics at each individual high schools varies, these tests provide colleges with students overall performance. The tests

171

were formulated by looking at the overall curriculum for high school students. Colleges have made these tests a frontrunner in their choice of admissions among students. While these test can be a decent predictor of a student's performance, they are not the most efficient way to determine admission consideration.

From my research I have discovered that there are many downfalls to standardized tests, and these will be the main focus of my paper. As stated in my thesis, standardized tests do not predict a student's accurate performance in college as well as does their high school GPA; they discriminate against minorities, and they have a negative effect on students, especially when overshadowing their overall high school performance. Being a student who has taken these tests, I have formed my own opinion about this topic that will also be incorporated in my paper. On top of my own thoughts and opinions, my research has helped to affirm my stance on this issue and provide many different reasons as to why the tests should be eliminated from academic consideration.

Organization and Schedule:

Outline:

- **INTRO:**
  - o Real life story to catch readers attention
  - o My background with the tests
  - o Thesis: Standardized Test Scores, such as the ACT and SAT, should be eliminated from the college admission requirements because they do not predict a student's accurate performance in college as well as their high school GPA, they are discriminative against minorities, and they have a negative effect on students, especially in their overall high school performance.
- **BODY PARAGRAPH 1: GPA has been proven to predict how a student will perform in college better than standardized tests**
  - o Show evidence
  - o Positives/ negatives of claim

- **BODY PARAGRAPH 2: Scores are also used for scholarships, which effect minorities who statistically perform worse on exams.**
  - o Evidence
  - o Examples
- **BODY PARAGRAPH 3: The effect standardized tests have on their high school student test takers.**
  - o Thoughts/feelings/stress
  - o Survey Answers
  - o Evidence of effect on high school performance during test taking time.
- **BODY PARAGRAPH 4: positives and negatives of dropping tests or using alternative routes in admission process**
  - o Give examples of schools
  - o Positives of the Standardized tests=negatives of dropping them
- **CONCLUSION:**
  - o Alternatives to testing
  - o Restate Thesis

Timeline:

- Continue researching
- Send email to class with survey questions about the ACT/SAT
- Calculate findings from surveys and summarize them
- Organize research into outline of paper
- Start drafting

Taylor Smith

Professor Malek

Engl 102.006

23 January 2012

Annotated Bibliography

Green, Raymond J., and Sandy Kimbrough. "Honors Admissions Criteria: How Important
Are Standardized Tests?" *Journal of The National Collegiate Honors Council* 9.2 (2008):
55-58. Education Research Complete. Web. 18 Jan. 2012.

"Honors Admissions Criteria: How Important are Standardized Tests" is a scholarly
journal article written by Raymond Green and Sandy Kimbrough. Green and Kimbrough
reviewed the entrance requirements for ten honors colleges in the south. Their goal was to
find the relationship between admissions criteria and first-year academic success. Through
their research they discover several findings related to standardized testing and GPA and
how they correlate to a students' performance as a first-year college studenst.

Although this article focuses on admissions to honors programs and not regular
admission into a University, the information it gives will still help in my arguments, and
further, will show how standardized test scores affect not only regular admission, but honors students, too. It gives information on what criteria predicts best academic success in
college, which will be one of the main parts of my paper.

Hoover, Eric. "DePaul U. Will make SAT and ACT Optional." *The Chronicle of Higher Education*. 00095982 (2011): n/a,n/a. *ProQuest Research Library.* Web. 18 Jan. 2012.

This news article written by Eric Hoover from The Chronicle of Higher Education
is saying that Depaul University is eliminating standardized-test scores as a requirement
for admissions. This decision was made because admission officers decided that "test
scores did little to help them predict student success beyond what high-school transcripts

revealed" (Hoover). This decision will make DePaul the largest private nonprofit university to go completely "test optional."

This article will serve as an example of an actual university putting into play the new admissions criteria of eliminating standardized tests. It will help give reasons why eliminating the tests is a good idea, while providing positives and negatives of the change.

Nicholson, Adelaide M. "Effects of Test Anxiety on Student Achievement (ACT) for College Bound Students." Trevecca Nazarene University, 2009. United States -- Tennessee: *Pro-Quest Dissertations & Theses (PQDT); ProQuest Dissertations & Theses A&I; ProQuest Dissertations & Theses A&I*. Web. 2 Feb. 2012.

Adelaide Nicholson's, "Effects of Test Anxiety on Student Achievement (ACT) for College Bound Students," provides information about a study done to test student's testing anxiety. During the tests, Nicholson found that "[m]any students anguish and stress over the thought of having to prove what they have learned academically while under pressure, unfamiliar with the test, in a foreign setting, and under time restraints" (2). Test anxiety leads to increased breathing and nervousness, worry and self-doubt. Self-doubt can be defined as the "I went blank" phrase in which self-doubt interferes with the problem solving abilities, which causes the thought process to be interrupted or not fully utilized to its full potential. In addition to stress, students also get test anxiety from parental pressure, peer pressure to do well on the exams, and competition for scholarships and financial aid based on test scores. Test anxiety is a major problem among students.

This article will help with me talk about the effect standardized tests have on students. It gives the solid example of test anxiety while providing reasons why standardized tests should be eliminated, especially for the students' well-being.

"Panel Urges Reduced use of College-Admission Exams." Education Week 28.6 (2008):

   13,n/a. *ProQuest Research Library.* Web. 18 Jan. 2012.

   In Kathleen Kennedy Manzo's article, the Commission on the Use of Standardized

Tests in Undergraduate Admission is recommending that colleges consider dropping the

tests as an entrance requirement. The article provides several positives and negatives of the

tests and gives alternatives to new criteria colleges might try in the future.

   This article will provide me with a strong case from a national organization to sup-

port my thesis that standardized tests should be eliminated and why it should be done. It

gives several viewpoints abot why students don't like the tests and the effects the SAT/ACT

have on their actual high school performance. The alternatives they give will also help in

wrapping up my paper.

"Planning for Imminent Change in College Admissions: Research on Alternative Admission

   Criteria." *Journal of College Student Retention* 1.1 (1999): 83-92. *ProQuest Research

   Library.* Web. 18 Jan. 2012.

   The scholarly journal article, "Planning for Imminent Change in College Admis-

sions: Research on Alternative Admission Criteria," consists of many different parts includ-

ing an abstract, and methodology, results, and conclusion sections. In the abstract, it refers

to two controversies that have occurred due to certain college admission criteria including

Proposition 209 in California and the Hopwood case. This article explains tests that have

been done as to why GPA is more important in college admission considerations than ACT/

SAT scores. In the results section, it provides charts with the results on the studies. Overall,

it shows the viewpoint of being against SAT/ACT scores for college admission.

   This source gives solid background about the SAT/ACT that will contribute to giving

my paper more depth. The tests and results of this article will help in my argument as to

why high school GPA means more than SAT/ACT scores in college admissions.

Selingo, Jeffrey. "Civil-Rights Groups Blast Florida's use of SAT Scores in Awarding Scholarships." *The Chronicle of Higher Education* 48.17 (2001): A.18-A18. *ProQuest Research
Library*. Web. 18 Jan. 2012.

This news article explains how the standardized test scores are used not only for
admission into colleges, but also for scholarship consideration. It focuses on the minority controversy over standardized tests. Because students from minority groups tend to do
worse on the SAT/ACT tests, civil-rights groups and educators think students are disadvan-
taged on college admissions and scholarships as well. Civil-rights groups in Florida are
asking Governor Jeb Bush to change the criteria for the state's merit-based scholarships
because the eligibility is based on "rigid test score cutoffs," a decision that tends to discriminate against minority students.

This article can also contribute to my argument stating that test scores affect more
than college admissions for students. This source talks about how standardized test scores
affect minority students when being chosen for scholarships, etc. The article will help give
a good solid example to my argument while providing statistical information to back it up.

Taylor Smith

Professor Malek

English Comp 102.006

Research Paper

12 March 2012

Standardized Tests: Every High School Student's Biggest Enemy

Uncomfortable in a wooden chair, I sat with a pencil in my hand. My mind attuned itself to the creaks of sliding chairs, the cracks of broken pencil tips, the rubbing of pink erasers, and the tapping of anxious feet. The clock beat louder than ever. I rubbed my head and bit my nails in hope of solving this riddle. I felt like a robot as I attempted to fill in hundreds of perfectly shaped bubbles. If only I were a wizard at puzzles and read 1,000 words per minute, there is no doubt that I would have achieved a perfect score on the SAT. I can say that "I am not a good test taker," or "English is not my best subject," or even "I like to read slow," but the SAT is unforgiving. Ultimately, that 3 or 4 digit number you achieve on the SAT will most likely determine which university you can and cannot go to and how much scholarship money you will receive. For universities the SAT and ACT is an easy, inexpensive, and accurate factor, yet to many students the SAT is an unfair representation of the student's gained knowledge and intellect.

Originally, colleges used standardized tests to avoid the hassle of having individual entrance exams for each school, while providing the academic capabilities of a student. According to researchers D. Tyson Bennet, Homer "Bucky" Wesley and Marion Dana-Wesley, "Standardized college entrance exams, such as the ACT and SAT were initially developed to avoid separate institutional tests and the ranking of individual high schools, and were designed to provide some degree of selectivity in the admissions process," which is why schools began to heavily rely on exam scores to determine school admissions. Colleges now use the scores as a foundational basis in deciding admission of students. Standardized testing is a major controversy among several different groups including universities,

178

students, teachers, parents and minorities. While these tests provide a decent prediction of a student's performance, they are not the most effective way to determine admission considerations. Standardized test scores, such as the ACT and SAT, should be eliminated from the college admissions requirements because they do not predict a student's accurate performance in college as well as their high school grade point average (GPA) does; they are discriminative against minorities, and they have a negative effect on those students who take the tests.

Through much research and a variety of tests and experiments, it has been proven that GPAs predict better how a student will perform in college in comparison to standardized tests. In "Honors Admissions Criteria: How Important are Standardized Tests," a scholarly journal article, Raymond Green and Sandy Kimbrough present their study of admissions criteria and first-year academic success. Green and Kimbrough reviewed the entrance requirements for ten honors colleges in the south. Through their research they discovered several findings related to standardized testing, GPA, and the correlation to a student's performance as a first-year college student. The article begins with background from studies previously performed which focus on the issue of what criteria for college admissions best predicts student success. The authors remain very neutral throughout the entire article stating their results of both positives and negatives of test scores, while also stating their main point that high school class rank percentile and GPA were stronger predictors in academic success of students. Through their studies, Green and Kimbrough found that "the correlations between high school class rank percentile and GPA were stronger than the correlations with standardized test scores" (Green and Kimbrough). Overall, they found that "class rank percentile is a good predictor of academic success for first year students. Individuals with lower class ranks, regardless of their standardized scores, were less likely to remain in the program" (Green and Kimbrough). Even though the findings are biased against using standardized test scores in the admissions criteria, the authors admit that "it would be premature to throw out standardized tests as part of the admissions process," because the study was only focused on first year college students (Green and Kimbrough). Furthermore, Green and Kimbrough suggest that "it may be that the standardized scores will be good predictors of GPA for the remaining three years of college or will accurately predict other criteria of success." However, this statement can be contradicted by the fact that standardized test scores are predictors of entering freshman, not how they will perform throughout their four years in high school. That being said, even though the study only covers the results of first year college freshman, it is still effective because standardized tests should only be used as a prediction of the first year.

Even the creators of the ACT and SAT, The College Board and the American College Testing Program, "affirm that performance in high school is the best predictor of academic success in college" ("Planning"). This affirmation was probably based on studies which prove that performance in high school overall and core GPA were relatively identical in variability and the largest contributors to overall college GPA ("Planning"). While talking with Paula LaManna from the admissions office here at the University of Cincinnati, she said that for admissions consideration they like to see a 2.7 cumulative GPA with a 21 ACT/980 SAT score. They also review class rank, courses completed in high school, and the essay and activity list, but GPA and test scores are given the highest priority. These requirements vary depending on the discipline applied to, such as DAAP. When applying to UC, I applied as Fashion Major in DAAP and did not even get considered because of my low ACT score. I found this extremely unfair especially because of my background in fashion design through my high school. If DAAP closely considered the high school I attended, they might realize that I would be a very successful candidate for DAAP. Unfortunately, test scores do not show your creative side. Furthermore, in a survey taken in my English class, one of my classmates stated that she did not do well on her tests but had an above average GPA in high school and is continuing that in college. Emphasizing the unfair advantage of standardized tests, she admits that she is not a good test taker and her performance is better reflected in her GPA. Although GPA should be of upmost importance in college admissions because of its ability to better predict college success, solely using GPA would have some negative effects:

> Considering only high school GPA without regard for the difficulty of competition, curriculum, and quality of education provided to the student, [which] would lead to inconsistent and inefficient admission review. Marginal students may complete the admission screening process with an adequate high school overall GPA, yet never been exposed to course designed to prepare them for college level work. ("Planning")

If test scores were eliminated then schools would need to consider looking at GPA much more closely to determine that students are coming from school with a good educational background. Although high school GPA is a solid predictor in academic success in college, it may be beneficial to use it in combination with other predictors apart from ACT and/or SAT.

Standardized test scores are not only important in admissions consideration, but also for many scholarships, awards, and incentives. Placing such an emphasis on standardized tests creates an unfair disadvantage for minorities who statistically perform worse on the exams. If "standardized exams have been associated with poor construction and administration, unreliability, and racial, cultural, class, and gender bias" ("Planning"), then why do colleges even bother using these exams? The fact that colleges put such great emphasis on test scores not only for admission consideration but also for scholarships is unfair and unethical to minorities. The article "Planning for Imminent Change in College Admissions: Research on Alternative Admission Criteria," provides the overall results of the 1997 SAT and ACT, which show how minorities tend to perform worse on the exams: For the SAT, African American test takers scored 12.2 percent lower than whites; females scored 2.5 percent lower than males; and test takers from the lowest socioeconomic status scored 16.1 percent lower than test takers from the highest SES category. The numbers for the results of the ACT vary slightly but their message remains the same: "They are seeing alarming tendencies in the exams, as evidenced by obvious disparities among the races, genders, and test taker's (household) socioeconomic status" ("Planning").

These alarming statistics have created controversy within minority groups. Jeffrey Selingo's article, "Civil-Rights Groups Blast Florida's use of SAT score in Awarding Scholarships," gives an example of the measures minority groups have taken to get rid of standardized test scores. Selingo writes that advocacy groups in Florida sent a letter asking Governor Jeb Bush to pressure colleges to reconsider their use of standardized test scores when awarding scholarships. Selingo states that, "black and Hispanic students are less likely than white students are to receive a merit award because minority students typically score lower than white students do on standardized test." Since statistics prove that minorities do worse on these exams, scholarships should offer a fair chance to everyone and eliminate the exams as the main factor in providing scholarships. It is the main factor because most scholarships require a minimum SAT/ACT score to even apply for the scholarship or be considered. Since minorities do worse, they often don't have these scores, and therefore aren't given their fair chance at them.

As a student who took the ACT and SAT twice each, I can only describe how nerve wracking it is even for the most confident students. Many thoughts and fears went through my head: fear of rejection, peer pressure, rising costs of college tuition, family legacies, and high anxiety. As students, we are taught that these scores basically determine our future: what college we will go to and what career we have. I always had the mindset that if you don't do well on your standardized tests, nothing else matters, no matter your performance in high school. My research has proven that this mindset is somewhat true. Nicholson in her article "Effects of Test Anxiety on Student Achievement (ACT) for College Bound Students," writes that during the tests "many students anguish and stress over the thought of having to prove what they have learned academically while under pressure, unfamiliar with the test, in a foreign setting, and under time restraints" (2). All of which lead to negative test scores that do not reflect the actual academic capabilities of the student.

As previously stated, although colleges do not use test scores exclusively, they do emphasize them because colleges think standardized tests are a good indicator of the academic potential and students abilities. A study was done in which researchers identified and studied the effects of test anxiety on student achievement as measured by the ACT for high school students who were college bound (Nicholson 4). They found that test anxiety leads to increased breathing and nervousness, worry and self-doubt, which causes thought processes to be interrupted or not fully utilized to its full potential (Nicholson 7). Test anxiety causes several negative affects on even the most scholarly of students. Nicholson cites a study by Mulvenson, Stegman, & Ritter in 2005, which noted the following:

> Test anxiety can affect any student, even at the highest level. National news sources report that the impact of standardized testing reveals many test-anxious students experience illness and increased levels of stress, both of which are attributed to the emphasis and administration of these tests. (8)

In addition to stress, students also get test anxiety from parental and peer pressure to do well on the exams, as well as competition for scholarships and financial aid based on test scores. Test anxiety is a major problem because, "these fears and anxieties are emotional problems, which if not addressed could result in decreased success in examination situations" (Nicholson 8). Obviously, if a student has anxiety or stress they will perform worse on the standardized tests. This is another issue in the test's ability to predict students' abilities, whereas GPA shows the students abilities over a four-year time span, under less stress, and in a familiar setting.

Many schools have implemented new strategies in their admission requirements, placing less, if not any, emphasis on standardized test scores: "280 out of 1,500 surveyed four-year public colleges and universities are not using the ACT or SAT in their admissions decision processes" ("Planning"). For example, according to Eric Hoover's article "DePaul U. Will Make SAT and ACT Optional: Applicants may choose to write essays that reveal 'heart'," DePaul University is eliminating standardized-test scores as a requirement for admissions. This decision was made because admission officers "decided that test scores did little to help them predict student success beyond what high-school transcripts revealed" (Hoover). This decision will make them the largest private nonprofit university to go completely "test optional."

By incorporating noncognitive variables, such as essays, DePaul finally came to the conclusion that "nontraditional measures did more than the ACT or SAT to predict the success of low-income and minority students at the university" (Hoover). Because of these findings, for those students who do not submit test scores, DePaul is now requiring short responses to essay questions designed to measure leadership, commitment to service, and ability to meet long-term goals. The credibility of DePaul University's decision is affirmed in the statement, "ACT and SAT scores are also solid predictors, they provide little additional insight beyond what a students high-school transcript reveals" (Hoover). DePaul hopes that the new policy will encourage prospective students to apply and convince them that their high school records matter more than their performance on the ACT or SAT. In Hoover's article, Associate Vice President for enrollment management, Jon Boeckenstedt, makes a solid point on his stance when he says, "Test scores are valuable for some things, but the focus and obsession we have about them as a country is a little bit misplaced, if not a lot misplaced" (Quoted in Hoover).

Even in the alternatives, like that exampled by DePaul University, there are some negatives to the elimination of standardized test from the admissions requirements. In their article, Bennett and Wesley state that, "Exam scores served as an objective screen for inflated GPA…" which implies that students with a low high school GPA, but high test scores, the standardized tests would be a plus. In DePaul's case, students may choose to submit test scores if they think their GPA is less sufficient then their ACT/SAT scores. With that consideration, I think schools should not fully eliminate the standardized test scores, but like DePaul University, make them an option for students.

Through much research and consideration of many options, it is clearly evident that standardized test scores, such as the ACT and SAT are not solid predictors in a students academic success in college because, as Bennett and Wesley's stated, they "have been associated with poor construction and administration, unreliability, and racial, cultural, class and gender bias" ("Planning"). Universities need to put less, if any, emphasis on the importance of the ACT and SAT in their college admissions requirements. Doing so will be advantageous for the colleges, as well as the students applying. Getting rid of standardized tests overall, or emphasizing their importance less, and concentrating more on high school GPA will eliminate discrimination among minorities, provide less stress and anxiety on test taking students, and offer a better consideration of students through alternative admission requirements.

Works Cited

Green, Raymond J., and Sandy Kimbrough. "Honors Admissions Criteria: How Important Are Standardized Tests?." Journal Of The National Collegiate Honors Council 9.2 (2008): 55-58. Education Research Complete. Web. 18 Jan. 2012.

Hoover, Eric. "DePaul U. Will make SAT and ACT Optional." *The Chronicle of Higher Education* (2011). *ProQuest Research Library*. Web. 18 Jan. 2012.

Nicholson, Adelaide M. "Effects of Test Anxiety on Student Achievement (ACT) for College Bound Students." Trevecca Nazarene University, 2009. United States -- Tennessee: *ProQuest Dissertations & Theses (PQDT); ProQuest Dissertations & Theses A&I*. Web. 2 Feb. 2012.

"Panel Urges Reduced use of College-Admission Exams." *Education Week* 28.6 (2008): 13. *ProQuest Research Library*. Web. 18 Jan. 2012.

"Planning for Imminent Change in College Admissions: Research on Alternative Admission Criteria." *Journal of College Student Retention* 1.1 (1999): 83-92. *ProQuest Research Library*. Web. 18 Jan. 2012.

SELINGO, JEFFREY. "Civil-Rights Groups Blast Florida's use of SAT Scores in Awarding Scholarships." *The Chronicle of Higher Education* 48.17 (2001): A.18-A18. *ProQuest Research Library*. Web. 18 Jan. 2012.

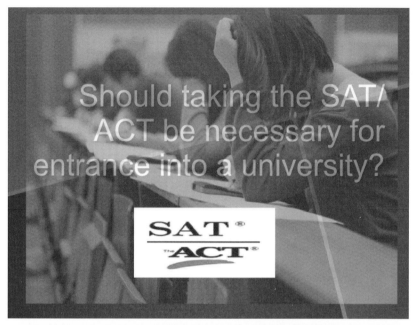

Should taking the SAT/ ACT be necessary for entrance into a university?

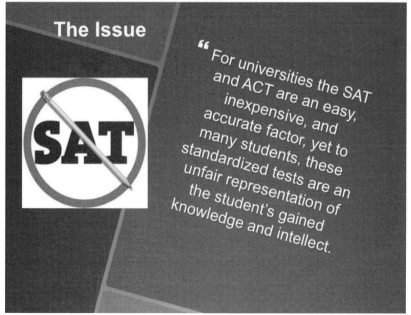

The Issue

" For universities the SAT and ACT are an easy, inexpensive, and accurate factor, yet to many students, these standardized tests are an unfair representation of the student's gained knowledge and intellect.

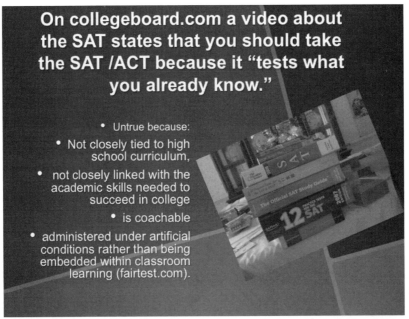

On collegeboard.com a video about the SAT states that you should take the SAT /ACT because it "tests what you already know."

- Untrue because:
- Not closely tied to high school curriculum,
- not closely linked with the academic skills needed to succeed in college
- is coachable
- administered under artificial conditions rather than being embedded within classroom learning (fairtest.com).

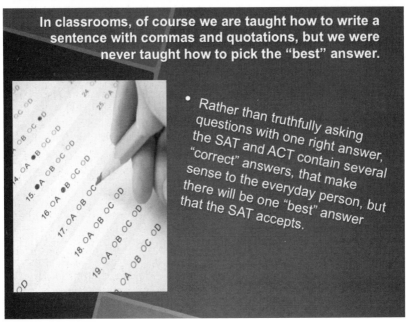

In classrooms, of course we are taught how to write a sentence with commas and quotations, but we were never taught how to pick the "best" answer.

- Rather than truthfully asking questions with one right answer, the SAT and ACT contain several "correct" answers, that make sense to the everyday person, but there will be one "best" answer that the SAT accepts.

CollegeBoard also states "It's fair to everyone," and "each question is tested to make sure all students from all backgrounds have an equal chance to succeed"

" Fairtest.org states that the SAT and ACT consistently **underpredicts the performance of females**. Although females earn higher grades in high school and college than males, their SAT scores were 26 points lower in 2006.

" Analyses of SAT/ACT gender bias show that females score lower because of the test's emphasis on speed over sustained reasoning and its multiple-choice format.

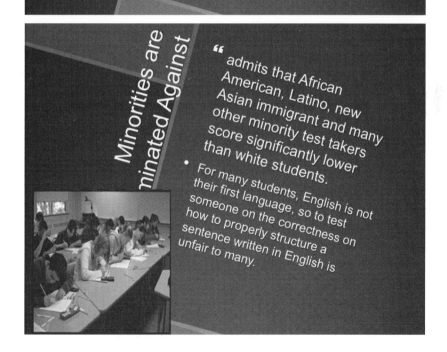

Minorities are ...minated Against

" admits that African American, Latino, new Asian immigrant and many other minority test takers score significantly lower than white students.

- For many students, English is not their first language, so to test someone on the correctness on how to properly structure a sentence written in English is unfair to many.

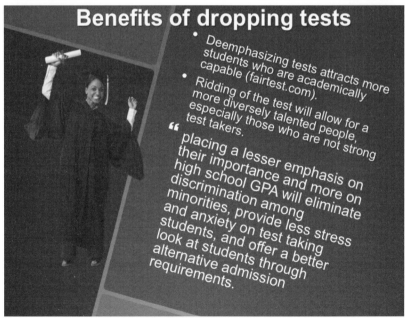

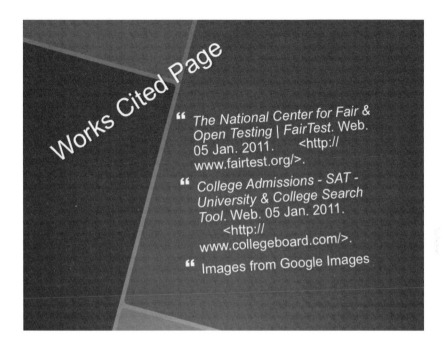

Taylor Smith

Professor Malek

English 102.006

9 March 2012

Rationale for PowerPoint presentation questioning whether or not the ACT and SAT should be necessary for college admissions

Background:

Today, several colleges and universities use standardized tests, such as the SAT and ACT as a strong determiner as to whether or not a student should be admitted into their school. For universities the SAT and ACT are an easy, inexpensive, and accurate factor, yet to many students, these standardized tests are an unfair representation of the student's gained knowledge and intellect, therefore they should not be used when considering a student's eligibility for admission into a university.

Purpose:

The purpose of my recast is to reach out to an adult audience through the presentation of a PowerPoint regarding the question of whether or not standardized tests, specifically the SAT and ACT, should be necessary for entrance into a university. Many colleges and universities are aware of the issues the SAT and ACT bring about. My presentation is to help further their understanding in these issues and realize they are not the right way for multiple reasons.

Audience:

I chose to focus on an audience of those working in college admissions, because I believe they would be the ones who will be able to make a change with this issue. They might also be unaware of the many benefits that come from dropping these tests. Although I know many students stand behind me in my argument and would do everything in their power to make a change, it is the college admissions officers who will be the most effective in changing college admissions requirements. Informing the people who have the authority to make changes regarding admissions requirements and standardized test scores will make my presentation the most effective.

Medium:

I chose to present my argument in the form a PowerPoint. Since my audience is college admissions officers, I felt a PowerPoint would be the easiest way to get their attention, while informing them at the same time. I chose to use a little information on each slide to be short and to the point. The different layouts, colors and pictures make my PowerPoint more interesting and easy to look at.

Discussion:

In order to get my points across clearly, but rapidly, I chose to use as few words as possible on my slides and to accompany them with as many pictures as I could provide. The images help balance some of my more text-heavy slides. The pictures bring color to the slides and make them more interesting to look at, allowing the words on the slide to be more enjoyable to read. I chose pictures to go along with the point I was trying to get across to my viewers. Since my topic is mostly information based, it was hard to intertwine pictures with them. Overall, I like the way the pictures I found connect with my statements and I feel it helps make my statements that much more powerful.

On the opening slide of my PowerPoint, I provided a picture of students taking the standardized tests as an attention getter to my audience. This picture is designed to remind them of students' test taking throughout the whole slideshow. My hope is that they will try to see the perspective of a student during my presentation. I also provided the emblem of the SAT and ACT tests. On my second slide, which presents my thesis and issue, I chose to put the image of the crossed out SAT because it tells my viewers my stance on this topic- I am obviously against the taking of standardized tests. From the first two slides, the audience is aware of the direction and stance of my presentation.

193

The title of slide three is a statement from collegeboard.com, the official website of the SAT. The statement is a strong claim made by the site. I provide information as to why the statement is untrue, and my picture of the books backs up these claims. The statement "it tests what you should already know" is in fact proven untrue through the many offered SAT/ACT prep books, SAT/ACT questions of the day, and the $900 or more SAT/ACT Prep classes offered to many high school students. Like slide 3, slide 4 also provides an attention-grabbing headline stating the fact that students were never taught how to choose the "best" answer. Illustrating this point is the picture of the filling in of bubbles on the test answer sheet in which students are told to fill in the best answer, even though many of them may be correct.

To get my arguments across, I needed to back up my statements clearly on the slides. Although some may seem text heavy, it was necessary for my argument. Since my audience is college admissions officers, I thought using a lot of words was not such a bad idea because they will be interested more in the information, rather then the pictures.

Taylor Smith

Professor Malek

English Comp 102.006

12 March 2012

Reflection Essay

Reflecting on my Research

When I began my research project and pondered what topic I should choose, I was having difficulties. I knew I wanted to write about something I found interesting, but I needed something that had enough information to write six to eight pages on. Then it dawned on me. I should write about the ACT/SAT standardized test controversy. I knew this topic would be something I would enjoy writing about, and also would be something I could relate to. After doing my initial research in the library with my class, I began to find floods of information on my topic. Going to the library as a requirement with my class really helped to get me motivated to start my research early, rather than leaving everything until the last couple of weeks before it was due.

From there, I developed my thesis which states: standardized test scores such as the ACT and SAT should be eliminated from the requirements for college admissions because they do not predict a student's accurate performances in college as a well as their high school GPA does; they discriminate against minority students, and they have a negative effect on the students taking the test. This thesis stuck as my final thesis.

Through my thesis statement, I was able to develop my three main points for the body paragraphs: standardized tests do not predict a student's accurate performance in college as well as does their high school GPA; standardized tests discriminate against minority students, and standardized test negatively affect students who take them.

As a research step, I organized each of my main points into an outline and wrote down exactly what I wanted to say about each of them. I also put corresponding quotations from sources in each category. Making an outline really helped my paper to stay organized, pairing research with the claims I was making. After completing my outline, writing my paper came easy. I knew exactly what I wanted to say and how I wanted to incorporate my sources.

After getting feedback from my teacher, Dr. Malek, I realized I needed work on framing my sources, something that was very new to me. With some intense revising, I hope I accomplished correct framing and that my sources are all used correctly. This part of the paper was the biggest challenge for me. Once I understood what I needed to do though, I think I accomplished correct framing of my sources so they flow with my paper more clearly.

My favorite part of the research essay is my first paragraph. I begin my paper describing a real-life scene of a student taking a standardized test. I describe the student's thoughts, feelings, and the pressure the student feels. I feel this opening scene draws my readers in and makes them want to read more. I tried to be very descriptive in order to bring my readers into the mind of the student in the hopes that they will place themselves in the student's position since my paper is written from the point of view of the student.

Before taking this class, I was pretty confident in my writing abilities, especially in writing research papers because I had written my fair share of research papers in high school. This research paper, however, was definitely different from the ones I had written before in high school because I got to choose my topic. Being able to choose a topic and pursue it made my argument stronger because I was passionate about it. I also liked that we did our research paper in steps throughout the term. It was very helpful to get pieces of the paper done with specific due dates to keep me on top of my project.

As a class overall, English Composition 102 has taught me very valuable writing tactics that I will carry with me to future classes. One of the main lessons I am taking from this class is to do my papers in increments over a longer period of time so that when it comes to doing my final draft, everything will lay out perfectly for me.